HOW TO PLAY FROM A REAL BOOK

FOR ALL MUSICIANS

by Robert Rawlins

ISBN 978-1-61780-355-0

HAL•LEONARD®
CORPORATION

7777 W. BLUEMOUND RD. P.O. BOX 13819 MILWAUKEE, WI 53213

Visit Hal Leonard Online at
www.halleonard.com

CONTENTS

Chapter 5 – Bass Lines

Chapter 6 – Playing the Chords

Chapter 7 – Playing the Melody and Chords Together

Chapter 8 – Improvisation

Chapter 9 – Reharmonization

PREFACE

How to Play from a Real Book is written for all musicians. It covers many techniques for exploring, understanding, and performing the songs found in real books. You will learn how to analyze the form and harmonic structure, insert an introduction, interpret the melody, improvise on the chords, construct bass lines, voice the chords, add substitutions, and much more.

This book assumes no knowledge of theory beyond the ability to read music in both clefs, but it takes a theory-based approach. We all know stories of highly accomplished musicians who knew little or no theory. Good for them. It shows how natural aptitude, total immersion in the field, and years of commitment can pay off. But for those whose aural abilities have limitations, who don't play these songs on the gig every night of the week, and who happen to have other obligations in their lives, a theoretical background can be of tremendous help. By understanding how and why these songs work, you can "own" them and better explore many creative options.

Every instrumentalist or singer can profit from this book. It addresses many aspects of solo and small band performance that can improve your own playing and your understanding of what others are doing around you. Even if you never touch a bass in your life, knowing how bass lines work will help your ear hear the chords when playing with a rhythm section. Similarly, learning about chord voicings, comping rhythms, reharmonization, turnarounds, and Latin rhythms will all help you better understand and connect with the rhythm section.

Finally, every musician should be able to sit down at the keyboard and make sense of a tune. I provide many options for playing the chords and melody, and none require large hands or advanced keyboard skills. Nor do I recommend any particular style. If a two-beat rhythm with straight seventh chords is your thing, that's fine. Many great performances have required nothing more. If roots and fifths just bore you to tears and you need some dissonance in your chords, those voicings can be found here as well. Playing from a real book is all about options. The material presented here will offer you a full range of techniques that you can put to use right away.

– INTRODUCTION –
The History of Real Books

In the early 20th century, sheet music was immensely popular. Many homes and businesses owned pianos, and amateur performance was commonplace. Records did not surpass sheet music sales for typical songs until the 1920s, and if you had a million-seller hit before then, you were talking about sheet music. At first, typical sheet music contained the melody with lyrics set to an arrangement for the piano. Here is "You Made Me Love You," from 1913:

Melody instruments could easily enough adapt typical sheet music to their needs, but other chord instruments could not. Guitar and banjo, which were becoming increasingly popular, could make slight use of a piece of sheet music. Then, following the 1915 Panama Pacific International Exposition held in San Francisco, the ukulele (of all instruments!) became the rage. It was light, inexpensive, relatively easy to play, and it soon became an icon of the Jazz Age. Music publishers were quick to recognize the potential for sheet music sales to this market and adapted their products accordingly. By 1920, many sheet music arrangements also contained fingering diagrams (called chord grids) for the ukulele. Here is "On the Alamo," from 1922:

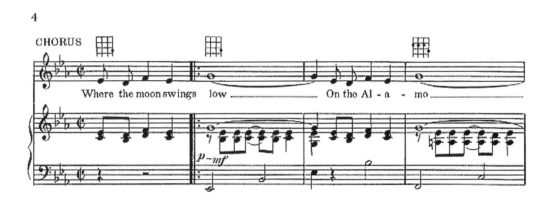

In an attempt to include other chord instruments as well, some publishers soon started adding both ukulele tablature and chord symbols. This would become the norm for the next several decades. Only from the 1950s on did guitar chord grids replace ukulele chord grids. Here is "Any Time," from 1921:

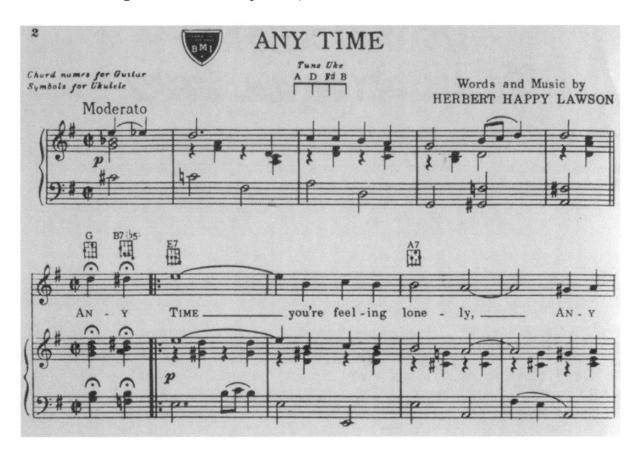

This evolution was by no means steady and consistent. Some publishers ignored the new notation completely, but by the 1930s grids and chord symbols were standard practice.

The problem was that the chords were not always meaningful representations of the harmonic movement of the song. Rather, they were simply an attempt to extract notes from the piano arrangement and show them as symbols. Sometimes this worked and sometimes it didn't. At its best, it more or less reflected the harmonic structure of the song. At its worst, it resulted in a desultory string of chords that might be passable in amateur performance, but made absolutely no musical sense as a harmonic progression. Musicians still refer to these haphazard sequences as "ukulele chords."

Sheet music posed other problems for the musician as well. Few professional musicians would be interested in the written piano score provided by sheet music, since it is stylistically nondescript and intended for solo performance. Moreover, the sheer number of pages involved, in addition to the expense of buying music by the song, made sheet music largely unpractical for the working musician.

So, musicians came up with their own way of writing out a song. They called it a "lead sheet." Typically, a lead sheet consists of a single line of music containing melody and chords (and possibly lyrics). If a musician didn't know a tune, he could always "fake it" by playing from a lead sheet. An early reference to a "fake book" was an advertisement for a company selling manuscript paper fitted into a loose-leaf binder, headlined "For Your Fake Book." The presumption was that you would write your own by hand.

The illegal fake books that sprang up in the 1950s are the ones all musicians know. Initially, these stemmed from a legitimate company called Tune-Dex, Inc. Between 1942 and 1963 the company printed and sold some 25,000 songs on 3 x 5 index cards with the melody and chords (to the chorus only) on one side and cataloging information on the other. Initially, the cards were intended to be used as a cataloging tool by a limited number of professionals in the music industry. But soon musicians found them indispensable, and the company did little to monitor or restrict its sales. Here is a Tune-Dex card, front and back:

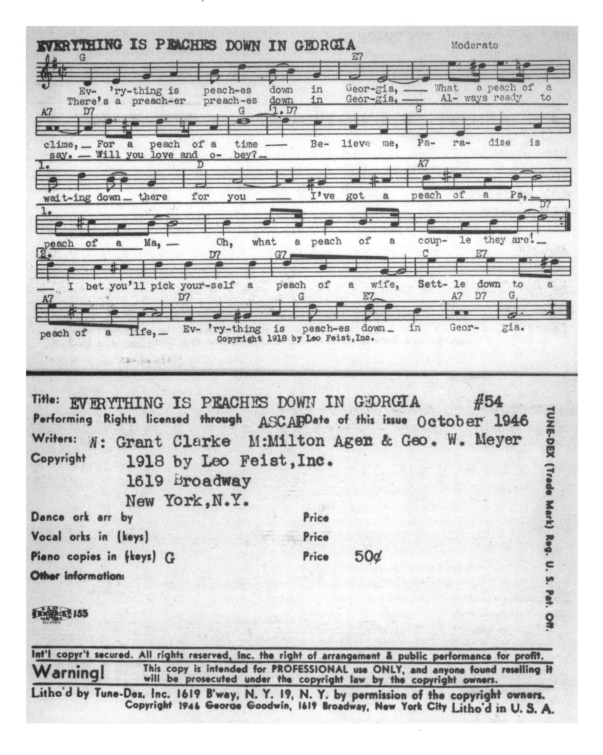

It was only a matter of time before someone got the idea that three of these could be printed on each side of a standard page, and that it would be relatively easy to assemble a fake book containing hundreds of songs in a modestly sized volume. Within a few short years, illegal fake books made from Tune-Dex cards had spread across the country, and there was little that law enforcement could to do to stop it. The few court cases that came up were half-hearted attempts to uphold the spirit of the law. It was obvious to everyone that musicians needed fake books for professional use, but because of the limited potential for sales, publishers were not filling this need.

By the 1960s, fake books of all kinds were being secretly printed and distributed under the counter. Many musicians considered them indispensible tools of the trade, since they had neither the finances to purchase thousands of copies of sheet music, nor the willingness to transport them to the job and wade through them for the necessary song. But fake books had issues other than copyright violation. They were often put together haphazardly, containing mistakes and poor chord choices.

In the late 1960s/early 1970s, a music publisher produced the first legal fake book, for which the song publisher and song writers were paid. By the mid-1970s, The Big 3 music publisher released a bigger and better legal fake book. Finally, in 1981, Hal Leonard Corporation published *The Ultimate Fake Book*, the best-selling legal fake book of all time. Hal Leonard followed with numerous other legal fake books, including *The Ultimate Broadway Fake Book*, *The Ultimate Country Fake Book*, *The Ultimate Jazz Fake Book*, and many others. These are currently available and continue to sell well.

In the mid-1970s, a collection of songs called *The Real Book* appeared on the scene. This contained jazz standards, as well as popular tunes commonly played by jazz musicians. It employed standard and consistent nomenclature for chord symbols, and included more accurate and advanced harmonies than typical fake books. (In other words, as the title suggests, this is what a fake book *really* should be.) In coming years, additional volumes of *The Real Book* were produced, but, as with many of the illegal fake books that came before them, they were still in violation of copyright law. Nevertheless, *The Real Book* became one of the most widely known and influential books in jazz. Moreover, its playful and poetic title introduced a new term into the musical lexicon.

In 2005, Hal Leonard Corporation published a legal edition of the original *Real Book*, soon followed by volumes II, III, and IV. Generally, a publisher will use the term real book to refer to a collection with more advanced harmonies, more specialized selections, strict adherence to the expectations of a particular style, or all of these things.

– CHAPTER 1 –
THEORY

"To study music, we must learn the rules. To create music, we must break them." – Nadia Boulanger

"I've found you've got to look back at the old things and see them in a new light." – John Coltrane

If you feel confident about your theory skills you might want to skip this chapter, but I'd suggest that you at least look it over. There are many approaches to music theory and different ways of viewing the same relationships. This chapter will help you better understand what's coming in the rest of the book. It's important that we're on the same page when we talk about chord symbols and what they designate.

Intervals

An interval is simply the distance between two notes. The smallest interval is the half step, which is the distance from one key to the next on the keyboard. As can be seen, a half step occurs between the white keys from E-F and from B-C. Other half steps require black keys. For example, C to C♯ is a half step.

A whole step is two half steps, or the distance between notes that are two keys apart on the piano. C to D is a whole step, as is E to F♯, or A♭ to B♭.

Intervals are generally measured by a number with a prefix. The number simply tells you the number of lines and spaces between the two notes, counting the starting note. Determining an interval's number is a rote process that does not require any calculation or observance of flats or sharps. For example, here are some intervals labeled by number only:

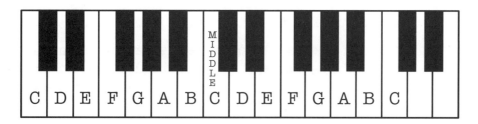

You really can't go wrong in finding the number for an interval. Just remember to count the starting note. Also, note that the piano won't help you here. Intervallic numbers refer to the staff, not the keyboard.

How high do the numbers go? For the purposes of chord building, they stop at 13. If for some reason you wanted to refer to a note 14 notes higher, you would say "an octave and a seventh."

Finding the prefix that qualifies the exact size of the interval is somewhat involved and derives from the traditional tonal system of Western music. If it did not, we could just count the number of half steps in an interval and be done with it. (This is done in some types of modern music.)

There are five basic terms that describe the quality of an interval: major, minor, perfect, diminished, and augmented. (The system is in fact open-ended in that we can continue expanding in either direction as much as we want by using the qualifiers "doubly diminished" and "doubly augmented." We could theoretically go beyond this with descriptors such as "triply diminished," but at that point the system becomes cumbersome and of little practical value.)

Here are the intervals with abbreviations that you may encounter:

Major   Maj, maj, M,

Minor   min, m, –

Perfect   per, P

Diminished   dim, d, o, ♭

Augmented   Aug, aug, A, +, ♯

As you can see, the symbols are not consistent and you are liable to encounter many variations. (This is especially true for complete chord designations.) If an interval number appears without a qualifier, perfect or major is assumed.

A good way to get a grasp of intervals is to derive them from the major scale. Below is a C major scale showing the sequence of whole and half steps. No matter what note you start on, a major scale will always have the same intervals in the same order. There will always be a half step between scale degrees 3-4 and 7-8.

The next step is to label the intervals that result in measuring from the starting note to each note in the major scale. Two different types of intervals result: major, designated by a capital M, and perfect, designated by a capital P.

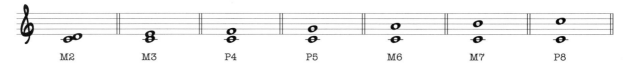

Observe that only seconds, thirds, sixths, and sevenths (as well as their compound relatives an octave higher) can be major. Only unisons (not shown), fourths, fifths, and octaves (along with their compound relatives) can be perfect. The take-home message here is that if you build all of the intervals in the major scale starting from the first note, you get major intervals except for the fourth, fifth, and octave, which are perfect. (They are called by that name because they were the first intervals to be used to harmonize Western music, and medieval music theorists considered their sound "perfect.")

The beauty of this major-scale approach to intervals is that if you know your major scales, you can quickly and reliably find any interval from the starting note. A perfect fifth up from A♭? E♭. A major seventh up from B? A♯. It's a fast and accurate system. But we still have other intervals to deal with.

Remember that as long as the notes of an interval stay on the same lines and space, the number of the interval can never change, no matter how much we change the size of the interval by adding flats or sharps. Only the quality changes. Here's how we can build any interval we need from a major or perfect interval:

perfect interval:	increased by half step	=	augmented interval
major interval:	decreased by half step	=	diminished interval
major interval:	increased by half step	=	augmented interval
major interval:	decreased by half step	=	minor interval
major interval:	decreased by whole step	=	diminished interval

Let's take some of the intervals we derived from the major scale and alter them into other intervals. Beginning with a perfect fifth, we can either raise the top note or lower the bottom note. In either case, we have expanded the perfect fifth by half step to make an augmented fifth.

P5   Aug5   Aug5

Now let's make the same interval diminished by reducing its size by half step:

P5   dim5   dim5

Expanding a major interval to an augmented:

M3   Aug3   Aug3

3

Or, reducing it to minor:

And diminished:

We've formed some very strange intervals here, but let's follow through and see how the system works. Normally, we don't need intervals like a diminished third when we can more easily write the interval as a major second. But as long as this interval is written so as to span three notes, it is a third and not a second and must be labeled as such.

The importance of being able to build intervals quickly and accurately cannot be overstated. The chords found in real books can be very complex, and there is no reason to memorize the content of each one as an independent entity. Rather, the trick is to be able to read the symbol and construct the chord by assembling its intervals.

Basically, any chord is a scale stacked in thirds rather than steps. Rarely will all the possible numeric intervals be present, but they are there nevertheless. Let's take a major scale and look at all the intervals that could occur by stacking the notes in thirds:

These are the important numbers involved in most chords—3, 5, 7, 9, 11, and 13. Chord symbols may refer to these intervals in varying ways, but the assumption is always that the unaltered intervals of the major scale are the starting point. Thus, a chord might call for a raised ninth, an augmented ninth, or a sharp ninth, but the supposition is always that something is being done to a major ninth.

Here's a good way to practice: Pick a key and go through intervals in your head. What's the 13th of an A♭ chord? The 11th? What's the ninth of an F♯ chord? The next step is to alter the notes. The 13th is naturally a major interval. So what's the ♭13 of an E♭ chord? The ♯11 of an F chord? You get the idea. Facility in building upward intervals is crucial to working with complex chords.

Extended chord tones can be calculated by subtracting the note degree by 7. Ex: 9th (-7) = 2nd
11th = 4th
13th = 6th

Chords: Construction and Function

A chord is a collection of notes played simultaneously, ranging from a simple dyad of two notes, through triads, sevenths, and extended chords, all the way to tone clusters with a potential twelve notes in them. In this book we will concern ourselves mainly with triads, seventh chords and extensions—that is, chords that derive from the traditional harmonic system.

Let's begin with triads—simple three-note structures. As can be seen, four triad types can be built by stacking major and minor thirds. (Although there are many ways to write the same chord symbol—more on that later—I've used three-letter abbreviations here for clarity.)

In a similar manner, we could construct all possible chords as independent stacks of thirds of various types, but that's not the best way to look at chords. To derive the most benefit from a real book, it is important to understand chord function as well as content. By "function," we refer to a chord's tendencies to progress to other chords. Why do we need to know this? For one thing, it's really the only way to memorize very complex tunes. For example, memorizing the chords to John Coltrane's "Giant Steps" would be a huge undertaking if you looked at the chords as a string of unrelated entities. But when you understand what's going on in the tune and see the very simple key and functional relationships, remembering the harmonic structure and even playing it in different keys is relatively simple.

For that reason, we will approach chords and function simultaneously. Let's begin with what I call the "diatonic array"—the collection of chords that occurs naturally from any scale when you stack notes in thirds. Here are the triads, with function:

Notice that all the notes used are contained in the major scale. No matter what key we do this in, we will get the same result—the same chord types of the same notes of the scale. We designate the chord built on a specific scale degree by using Roman numerals. Upper case numerals indicate major chords and lower case numerals minor chords. For diminished, augmented, and sevenths, other symbols have to be added.

Diatonic Seventh Chords: Major

Seventh chords provide the foundation of jazz harmony, just as triads provide the foundation of classical harmony. These are the commonly used seventh chords, with the symbols commonly used to designate them:

major seventh	M7, maj7, Δ7, Δ
minor seventh	m7, min7, –7
dominant seventh	7
diminished seventh	dim7, o7
half-diminished seventh	ø, ø7, min7(♭5), m7(♭5)
minor/major seventh	m(maj7), –maj7, –M7, mM7, –Δ
dominant seventh sus	7sus4, 7sus
dominant seventh (flat fifth)	7(♭5)
augmented seventh	+7, aug7, 7(♯5), 7(+5)

As you can see, the symbols are all over the place. Unfortunately, there is no "standard" imposed on how musicians should designate their chords. Even if there were, it's too late—there are thousands of books circulating with all of these chord symbols. The only thing to do is to learn all the possibilities and be able to recognize them. Here are the chords from above, spelled out with recommended symbols:

Just a few comments on this list: I've written the C°7 chord with B♭♭ to be technically correct, but practically everybody converts double flats or sharps to the equivalent note (A, in this case). Nevertheless—to honor the theory behind the chord—it consists entirely of minor thirds, and therefore requires a B♭♭.

The best way to think of a sus chord is as a chord where the fourth replaces the third. Although "sus" originally was an abbreviation for suspended, the contrapuntal background of this chord no longer applies. In other words, in classical music a suspended fourth must by definition be followed by resolution to a third. But this simply does not happen in jazz and popular music. A sus chord just sits there as an entity in itself, and therefore the word "suspension" is best avoided.

Classical musicians prefer the term (and symbol) "half diminished" to "m7♭5". However, the latter term better describes the function of the chord in modern contexts. That is, its function relates to that of a minor seventh chord, not to that of a diminished chord.

Let's have a look at the diatonic seventh chords and their functions:

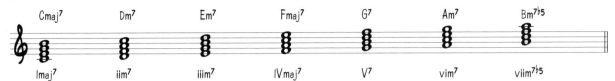

It would be good to pause for a moment and think about what we're doing here. We're taking a collection of seven notes (the C major scale) and giving each note in the scale a chance to be the starting note or root of a chord. As it works out, two of the notes yield major seventh chords (I and IV), three yield minor seventh chords (ii, iii, and vi), one gives us a minor 7♭5 (vii), and one gives us a dominant seventh (V).

This pattern will hold true for all keys, and it should be learned thoroughly. A good way to practice it is to pick a key, write the scale with accidentals, write the functions underneath, and then fill in the notes *without using the key signature*. For example, here is D♭ major:

Next, place the chord names on top:

And now fill in the notes:

Do this in every key a few dozen times and you'll really have a handle on it. The reason for not using a key signature is that you wouldn't really be doing anything except filling in the notes. This method makes you think.

For those familiar with triadic harmony but not familiar with harmony based upon seventh chords and extensions, this array of functions might seem daunting. The good news is that we rarely use more than three of the functions. Let's take a look at the major scale again and note where the half steps are:

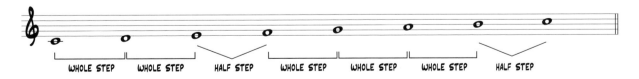

They are between scale degrees 3-4 and 7-8. Notes that are close to a potential note in the tonic chord have a strong tendency to resolve to that note. This works just like gravity or magnetic attraction. A note that is a half step away from what would be a note of resolution (C, E, or G in this case) wants to move to that slot. The short of this is that scale degrees 4 and 7 are "hot." They want to move, propel the music forward, or induce change, so that we get to a chord of repose. Of these two notes, the F is particularly powerful because downward resolution is stronger than upward. So let's look at our diatonic chords to see which ones contain the fourth:

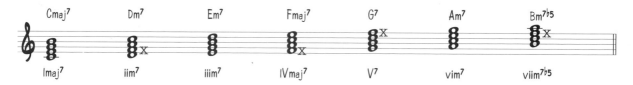

It is evident that Imaj⁷, iiim⁷, and vim⁷ do not contain the fourth scale degree. For this reason, we label them *tonic* chords. They are chords of rest and all are equivalent in terms of basic harmonic function. They can freely be substituted for one another. (See Chapter 9, Reharmonization.)

Of the four chords that do contain the fourth, we will make a further distinction: V⁷ and viim⁷⁽♭5⁾ contain both the fourth and the seventh scale degrees. Not only do these chords contain two tendency tones, but the two tones together form a dissonant interval that does not appear in the other chords. F to B is an augmented fourth, and its inversion, B to F, is a diminished fifth. Both are considered a tritone (meaning three whole steps), which is the most dissonant interval in music. We will call this category of chords *dominant* chords, because of their strong tendency to resolve to tonic chords.

The two remaining chords, iim⁷ and IVmaj⁷, which contain the fourth but not the seventh, express some tendency to resolve, but not as much as the dominant chords. They are, therefore, *pre-dominant* chords.

The seven diatonic chords in major thus fall into three families:

tonic	Imaj⁷, iiim⁷, vim⁷
pre-dominant	iim⁷, IVmaj⁷ — *subdominant*
dominant	V⁷, viim⁷⁽♭5⁾

The normal tendency of music follows a three-part scheme of pre-dominant, dominant, tonic. Choosing the progression that moves by the strongest root motion, perfect fourths and fifths, we get iim⁷–V⁷–Imaj⁷, the most common progression in jazz.

Diatonic Seventh Chords: Minor

Minor keys open up vast possibilities because of the "floating" sixth and seventh degrees, which can be natural or raised depending on the type of minor scale used. But the most common minor chords are built on the harmonic minor scale:

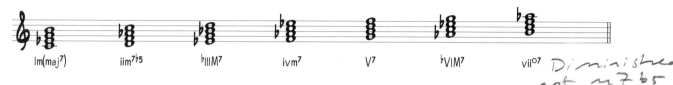

Im(maj⁷)   iim⁷♭5   ♭IIIM⁷   ivm⁷   V⁷   ♭VIM⁷   vii°⁷   *Diminished,*
not m7♭5

Notice the inclusion of a flat in front of IIIM⁷ and VIM⁷. The 3 and 6 of the scale are already lowered. Couldn't we could just call them III and VI without the flats in front of the symbol? We could, but since the sixth and seventh degrees of the minor scale could be either natural or flat, this could result in confusion with other chords build on these scale degrees. It's better to use the flats in order to be clear. *Nat minor: 1 2 ♭3 4 5 ♭6 ♭7*
mel minor: 1 2 ♭3 4 5 6 7

If we adhered strictly to the harmonic minor scale, ♭III would be an augmented chord with a major seventh (a rare bird in the repertoire). Therefore, the substitution of a straight major seventh chord is almost always used. Since the minor scale has variable sixth and seventh degrees, it is possible to construct several other chords. For instance, we could build a chord on the natural sixth or on the lowered seventh. But these chords do not come up as often and need not be considered at this point. *harm. minor: 1 2 ♭3 4 5 ♭6 7*

b/c aug is usually dominant

Minor key chord function groups are not as clear cut as in major, since more tendency tones are at work, but can be categorized as follows:

tonic   im(maj⁷), ♭IIImaj⁷, ♭VImaj⁷

                    (♭VImaj⁷ can also function as pre-dominant)

pre-dominant   iim⁷♭5, ivm⁷

dominant   V⁷, vii°⁷

The important thing to remember about functions in chord progressions is that jazz and pop tunes rarely stay in one key for very long. Modulation is rampant and chord functions are generally basic progressions that clearly define the key of the moment.

Chord Extensions

As was mentioned earlier, the seventh is not considered an extension in jazz, but rather a basic part of the diatonic harmony. Since seventh chords consist of four notes, we only have three scale degrees left to build extensions on—2, 4, and 6—which we will usually (but not always) call 9, 11, and 13.

Now here's the rub: We build our 7th chords by staying within the diatonic scale and avoiding sharps and flats. Except for a couple of modifications in the minor key, the triads with sevenths were what they were and we had no choice in the matter. That doesn't work for extensions.

For example, the tonic chord in C major is a Cmaj[7]. If we add the ninth that the scale gives us, we get a Cmaj$^{7(9)}$, which is fine. But if we add the 11th that the scale gives us—F, well, that's not fine. Remember our discussion about the fourth being a tendency tone and needing to resolve? Obviously, putting that note into the tonic chord—the chord of repose—is not going to work.

All the seventh chord types that we discussed can receive multiple extensions, but they cannot receive just any extensions. In truth, the available extensions were worked out by ear throughout the 20th century, and theoretical explanations lagged behind—if they developed at all. Following is a chart of extreme importance in reading from a real book. It lists the available extensions on all common chord types.

Before we present the chart, we need to add one piece of information to our list of diatonic chords: While Imaj[7] and im(maj[7]) are certainly options, in actual practice I[6] and Im[6] are at least as common. In other words, the 13th, by itself or with other notes, is so frequently added to these chords that it is designated as the sixth. Nothing else changes. Can both the sixth and seventh be present? Yes, but we would call that a seventh chord with a 13th. Just be aware that these chords may be used with the sixth (or 13th) *in place of* the seventh.

Here is the chart: *Memorize — + know how to form chords*

Chord Type	Available Extensions
C6	9, ♯11
Cmaj7	9, ♯11, 13
Cm6	9
Cmmaj7	9, 13
Cm7	9, 11, 13
Cm7♭5	9, 11, ♭13
C7	♭9, 9, ♯9, ♯11, ♭13, 13
C+7	9, ♯11
C°7	Any note a whole step above a chord tone (no numbers used)
C7sus	♭9, 9, 13

This chart covers the basics. Other options exist, and some of the ones I included require specific contexts, but the above guide will go a long way in providing reasonable choices for extensions.

Which Extensions and How Many?

Even the best real books are only guides and will not provide you with the extensions you need for a convincing performance of the song. Some provide more information than others, but in general, exact upper structures are included only if they are integral to the song. If you see simple triads, or only sixth and seventh chords, you can be sure that you're supposed to be choosing the extensions yourself.

How do you do that? There's a big difference between playing a basic triad or only chord and adding every available extension. Which ones you choose to add will depend on style and context as well as personal choice. Even Dixieland musicians will use upper extensions at times, while musicians with vast harmonic resources, such as Oscar Peterson or George Shearing, will make much use of simple triads and only chords. Variety is certainly a factor.

There's no rule for how many total notes a chord should have. You can use a fragment of a chord (say, seventh, ninth, and third), or as many notes as your fingers can lay down on the piano. You can double notes, or have chord tones represented just once. And you don't have to keep the same number of voices from chord to chord. Strict rules govern the way chord tones move in classical music, but those rules don't apply to jazz.

Before suggesting recommendations—and that's all they are—for upper extensions, we need to be clear on one point: Extensions do not have to be added in sequence from the bottom up. In other words, you don't need to have a ninth to add an 11th or 13th. (In fact, you don't even need the seventh, and triads with extensions of a ninth or beyond are rare but effective chord choices.) All choices are fair game, but all choices don't sound the same.

Major chords will usually be written as major sixths or major sevenths in real books. Generally, the melody of the tune determines that choice. If the melody emphasizes the major seventh, such as in "After You've Gone" or "The Girl from Ipanema," the chord will be a major seventh. If the melody is on the sixth, such as "My Ship," then the chord will be a major sixth. For all of the tunes that don't have a sixth or seventh steering the melody, the choice is really up to the performer. When the tonic is in the melody, some musicians prefer a sixth to avoid a clash. Others are not bothered by the dissonance between the major seventh and the root in the melody.

In most cases, a ninth will also be added to a major sixth or major seventh. A major seventh can stand alone pretty well, but a major sixth by itself will have a distinctive 1930s sound to it, which may or may not be what you want. A major seventh can also have a seventh, either with or without the ninth.

The ♯11 is not generally an option during the course of a tune unless it is part of the melody or character of the song. The reason is that it simply draws too much attention to itself. Therefore, unless the tune calls for it, avoid ♯11 chords except for final endings.

The minor sixth or min(maj7) chord is more dissonant than its major counterpoint and therefore requires fewer, if any, extensions. A minor 6/9 or a min(maj7) is generally all you need.

Minor seventh chords are very accepting of upper structures and generally receive the ninth, or both the ninth and 11th. The 13th is rare.

The minor7♭5, on the other hand, contains enough dissonance to stand on its own without extensions. The ninth is actually quite dissonant on this chord—more so than the 11th or ♭13. The reason is that the min7♭5 is often functioning as iim7♭5, meaning that the ninth is actually the major third in the minor key. Another reason for limiting extensions to this chord is that the fifth is integral to the sound. When a chord has a natural fifth, it is often omitted, since it does not affect the chord quality. But when the fifth is altered, it must be included.

11

Dominant seventh chords are capable of receiving the most extensions. Any note other than the major seventh and perfect 11th is possible. Generally, one or two extensions will be added:

Dominant Seventh Chord	Usage
V7 9 or V7 9,13 or V7 add 13	common, especially in major
V7♭9 or V7 ♭9, ♭13	common in both major and minor
V7 9, ♭13	common in both major and minor
V7 ♭9, 13	common in both major and minor
V7 ♯9 or V7 ♯9, ♭13	common in both major and minor
V7 ♯9, 13	usually only in blues contexts
V7 ♭9, ♯9	rare
V7 ♭9, 9 or V7 9, ♯9	not used
V7 ♭13, 13	not used

For added dissonance, or when the context calls for it, ♯11 can be added to any V7 chord. If ♯11 is used with both the ninth and the 13th, they will generally be "matched." (Both will be altered or neither.)

Dominant Seventh Chord	Usage
V7 9, ♯11, 13	common, especially in major
V7 ♭9, ♯11, ♭13	common in both major and minor
V7 ♯9, ♯11, ♭13	common in both major and minor
V7 ♭9, ♯11, 13	less common
V7 ♯9, ♯11, 13	less common
V7 9, ♯11, ♭13	rare

Augmented seventh chords are actually dominant chords. Since the fifth is often omitted from dominant chords, and always omitted when the ♭13 is present, the raised fifth and the ♭13 are the same. The reason for writing a chord as C^{+7} is that it specifically calls for whole tone scale, which is completed if 9 and ♯11 are added.

For older songs, four-note diminished seventh chords can be appropriate. For a more modern sound, you might want to add at least one extension to the chord. (The possible extensions for a diminished chord are the four notes one whole step above each chord tone.) With more than two extensions, a diminished seventh chord can begin to lose its identity. Also, in many instances, extensions will replace the note a whole step below, so that you still have a four-note structure.

Sus chords, like minor seventh chords, are very accepting of upper extensions. Add 9, 13 or both to enhance the quality of the chord. Another option is to add a ♭9. (This will sometimes be written as a minor chord with an added ninth. For example, $C^{7sus♭9}$, C-F-B♭-D♭ is the same as B♭m add 9, B♭-D♭-F-C.)

Limitations of Chord Symbols

A chord symbol is meant to supply crucial harmonic information, while leaving many choices for the performer. Symbols vary significantly in how much information they specify and how much they leave open. For example, some publications consistently indicate major chords as triads, not because they expect the performer to play triads, but because they don't want to specify any upper structures at all, even leaving the choice of using a major sixth or a major seventh up to the performer. Similarly, other chord types will be specified only up to the seventh, letting the performer make choices regarding the ninth, 11th, and 13th. Others will make suggestions for more specific chords—but it is important to understand that they are only suggestions. If jazz is about anything, it is about freedom.

Here are the opening bars to "My Ship." The first excerpt gives a bare bones approach to the chords, while the second gets more specific. Most people would probably play something more like the second excerpt anyway when reading from the basic chords, but this is by no means the only possible interpretation.

MY SHIP

Words by Ira Gershwin
Music by Kurt Weill

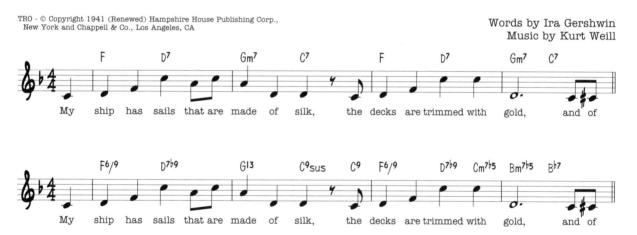

Slash Chords

Chord symbols are also able to specify bass notes; these are generally referred to as "slash chords." The letter to the right of the diagonal line indicates the bass note, while the chord symbol is interpreted in the usual fashion:

Dm9/G

Alternate bass notes can be indicated to change the quality of the chord or to ensure a smoother bass line. "My Buddy" is a tune that lends itself to slash chords. In the setting below, notice how the slash chords result in a smooth and logical bass line.

MY BUDDY

Lyrics by Gus Kahn
Music by Walter Donaldson

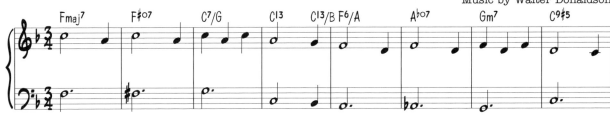

Polychords

The concept of polychords is employed more frequently by jazz musicians than it appears in chord symbols. As the term suggests, it involves combining two or more chords at the same time. Of course, with upper structures, this often occurs anyway. For example, Cmaj^9 contains both a C triad and a G triad. C$^{7\sharp 9}$ contains a C^7 chord and an E$\flat$ triad.

But a true polychord suggests a degree of independence between the two structures, implying that they are nearly of equal importance. For example, combining C and D triads into a polychord on the piano would probably require separating them between the two hands.

Polychords allow for a level of dissonance not usually possible through straight extensions. Because each structure implies a degree of cohesion and recognition by itself, there is an ambiguity going on when the chords are sounded together.

Polychords are represented in chord symbols by placing one chord over the other, separated by a horizontal line:

$$\frac{B}{Cmaj^7} \qquad \frac{A\flat}{C^7} \qquad \frac{F\sharp m}{C}$$

Add and Omit Chords

Occasionally a chord symbol will give specific instructions about which notes to include or omit when the chord produced is somewhat unusual. This is most commonly used when the chord calls for a triad with an upper structure but no sixth or seventh. But many other possibilities exist. Here are some examples:

The use of the "add" and "omit" qualifiers along with traditional chord symbols allow for the inclusion of practically any combination of notes.

This list is not exhaustive, but covers the most common chord types. Some of these chords are unusual, but are included to show how the symbols would indicate them:

Many more combinations of extensions are available on dominant seventh chords. Symbols follow similar patterns.

– CHAPTER 2 –
ANALYSIS AND WHY YOU NEED IT

"Good music never gets old." **– Jelly Roll Morton**

"Once I hear a good tune—if it's a good tune—I don't forget it."
– Eubie Blake

Chords do not exist as separate independent note collections on their own. They are vibrant parts of an entire composition that is unfolding in real time. In order to improvise effectively on a chord, choose appropriate upper structures, or decide on a chord voicing, it is necessary to know how that chord functions in the tune.

How is it possible for musicians to keep hundreds, perhaps thousands, of songs in their head and not get the chords confused? One way is to know them so thoroughly that the harmonies can be heard internally. But this chapter will provide a quicker method. By analyzing the chord sequences of a tune and understanding the basic layout, the harmonic structure can be learned within minutes—without ever hearing the song—and committed to memory rather easily. All you need to do is see the big picture.

Diatonic Progressions

The procedure for harmonic analysis is straightforward: Simply determine the key that a group of chords belongs to and assign the proper Roman numeral. It is customary to place the analysis below the chords or staff and to use a letter with a colon to designate the key. For example:

F^6	Dm^7	Gm^7	C^7
F: I^6	vim^7	iim^7	V^7

This progression, referred to as "one, six, two, five," is very common. It turns up again and again in all kinds of songs. Below is the beginning of "Beyond the Sea."

BEYOND THE SEA

Lyrics by Jack Lawrence
Music by Charles Trenet and Albert Lasry
Original French Lyric to "La Mer by Charles Trenet

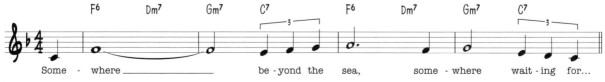

16

There are reasons why the I–vi–ii–V progression is so common. For one thing, it follows a normal perceptual expectation in building up tension and releasing it. Recall that we categorized I^7, $iiim^7$, and vim^7 as tonic chords (least tension), iim^7 and $IVmaj^7$ as pre-dominant chords (some tension), and V^7 and vii^{o7} as dominant chords (most tension). Also, presumably, a I chord will follow the V^7, so we start from a position of repose, gradually build the tension to a maximum, and then release. We normally expect this pattern and most music is based upon this understanding.

Also, notice that the progression from vi to ii to V to I involves motion by perfect fourth up or perfect fifth down. There exists a strong tendency for chords, no matter what their type, to follow this pattern. Here are all possible chord roots arranged in a Circle of Fifths. The normal progression of chords is counterclockwise around this circle.

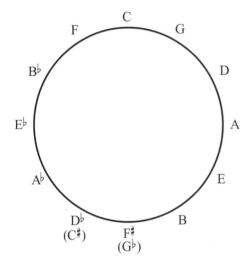

But of course chords do not always follow this pattern. Sometimes music is more interesting when it doesn't do what you expect it to.

Modulation

If all songs were confined to diatonic chords and remained in the same key throughout, then we could end this discussion here. We could just look at the key signature and assign one of the seven Roman numerals to each chord of the song. However, few songs do that. Most change key or *modulate*. For example, the bridge to "Beyond the Sea" modulates to A major. The key signature doesn't change, but the chords and melody clearly indicate that the song has shifted into a new tonal area:

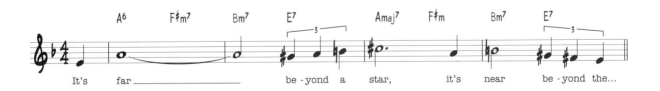

Again, the progression is I, vi, ii, V. Here is the analysis:

	A^6	$F\sharp m^7$	Bm^7	E^7
A:	I^6	vim^7	iim^7	V^7

Sometimes the new key is not so obvious. Following is a sequence of chords that moves through three different keys, with the analysis below:

Gmaj^7	Am^7	D^7	Gmaj^7	Dm^7	G^7	Cmaj^7	Am^7	Gm^7	C^7	F
G: Imaj^7	iim^7	V^7	Imaj^7	C: iim^7	V^7	Imaj^7	vim^7	F: iim^7	V^7	I

How did we know to change key for the Dm^7? Because there is no Dm^7 chord in the key of G. How did we know we modulated to C major? Because G^7 as a diatonic chord exists only in the key of C. Similarly, C^7 tells us we are going to the key of F, because no other key contains that chord.

The secret to determining what key a song modulates to from looking at the chords is to realize what keys those chords occur in. Remember, the diatonic array in major or minor can never change. You can't "force fit" a chord into a function that it doesn't belong to. And the ii–V progression is a real giveaway. Whenever you see a minor seventh chord followed by a dominant seventh chord a perfect fourth higher, you can be nearly certain that the progression is iim^7–V^7 in the key a perfect fifth below the dominant. In other words, "if it looks like a ii–V, it *is* a ii–V."

Secondary Functions and Tonicization

Modulations can be so brief that they do not even come to rest in the new key, in which case they are referred to as *secondary dominants* or *tonicizations*.

Duke Ellington's "In a Mellow Tone" (based on the chords to an older tune called "Rose Room") begins with a secondary dominant. The B♭^{7}, a dominant chord, clearly belongs to the key of E♭. But we never arrive in the key of E♭, because B♭^{7} resolves to E♭^{7}, which is the dominant chord in the key of A♭.

IN A MELLOW TONE

By Duke Ellington

We analyze a secondary dominant chord with a slash, which in this case is read as "five of five." That is, the first chord is the dominant of the dominant (V/V).

	B♭^{7}	E♭^{7}	A♭maj^7
A♭:	V^7/V	V^7	Imaj^7

Agua De Beber

Amin^7 · B7#9 · E7#5

Amin: im^7 · V^7/V · I^7

Secondary dominants can occur in sequence—each implying the key a perfect fifth below, only to resolve to another secondary dominant implying the perfect fifth below that. Successions of dominant chords were widely used in songs of the first half of the 20th century. Below is a tune from 1921, "There'll be Some Changes Made." Notice that a Circle of Fifths dominates the tune, and the tonic chord is not heard until near the very end.

THERE'LL BE SOME CHANGES MADE

Words by Billy Higgins
Music by W. Benton Overstreet

Since it is obvious what is going on in such a tune, it is seldom necessary to analyze every chord. But if you did, the first half would look like this:

	G^7	C^7	D^7	G^7	C^7	Cm^7	F^7
$B\flat$:	V^7/ii (C)	V^7/V (F)	V^7/vi (G)	V^7/ii (C)	V^7/V (F)	iim^7	V^7

↳ secondary dominant of the ii

Such progressions are common in the Dixieland repertoire and there are many Dixie tunes that consist primarily of dominant chords. Since they almost always resolve down a fifth, all you need to do is remember where to "get on," and then just ride the cycle.

Also, note the inclusion of the Cm^7 in measure 8. If one or more chords intervene before the resolution of the secondary dominant, nothing is changed. In other words, the C^7 in measure 7 is still "looking at" the F^7 in measure 8. The Cm^7 occurs in between but does not interrupt the harmonic flow.

Secondary ii–V progressions are classified as tonicizations, meaning that a key area is hinted at but not actually established. Analysis is usually shown with a horizontal line:

	$Fmaj^7$	$Am^7\flat5$	$D^7\flat9$	Gm^7	C^7
F:	$Imaj^7$	$iim^7\flat5$	$V^7\flat9$	iim^7	V^7
		iim^7			

↳ Gm

Sometimes you will see a series of ii–V progressions, each leading to the next in a continuous cycle:

	Bm^7	E^7	Am^7	D^7	Gm^7	C^7	$Fmaj^7$
F:	iim^7	V^7	iim^7	V^7	iim^7	V^7	$Imaj^7$
	iii		ii				
	A		G				

In other instances, ii–V⁷ progressions seem to be random, yet permeate the song, as in John Coltrane's "Lazy Bird":

LAZY BIRD

By John Coltrane

How do you memorize a progression such as this? Actually, it's not as hard as you might think. Once you understand the premise behind the tune, it becomes relatively easy to reproduce it in any key with little effort. But to understand how this tune is constructed, we need to introduce a few more concepts.

Borrowed Chords and Keys

Aside from secondary functions and modulations, even when in the home key, we are not confined to the diatonic chords. It is also possible to use chords "borrowed" from the parallel minor or major key. Consider Louis Armstrong's "Swing That Music." Why the IV⁷ in measures 3 and 4, when in a major key you would expect IVmaj⁷? The answer is that it is borrowed from the key of B♭ minor where IV may be a dominant seventh chord. (IV may also be a minor chord in a minor key—and that borrowing is common as well.)

minor = the IV can be Dom or minor
key

SWING THAT MUSIC

Words and Music by Louis Armstrong
and Horace Gerlach

My heart gets a chill, ___ I feel such a thrill, ___ my...

Bb: I   IV7

In the second bar of "After You've Gone," we see an example of iv borrowed into a major key:

AFTER YOU'VE GONE

Words by Henry Creamer
Music by Turner Layton

Af-ter you've gone, and left me cry-ing, af-ter you've gone, ___ there's no de-ny-ing,

Bb: IV   iv   I   V7/ii

Any minor diatonic function can be pulled into a major context. (Borrowing from the major when in minor can happen, but it is rare. One relatively common occurrence is to end on a major chord when in a minor key.)

Here is a list of chords that are routinely borrowed from the minor:

- iim7b5
- IIImaj7
- iv7
- IV7
- VImaj7
- bVIImaj7
- vii°7

With the possibilities of borrowing chords—or entire key areas—from the minor, the structural design of "Lazy Bird" makes perfect sense:

LAZY BIRD

By John Coltrane

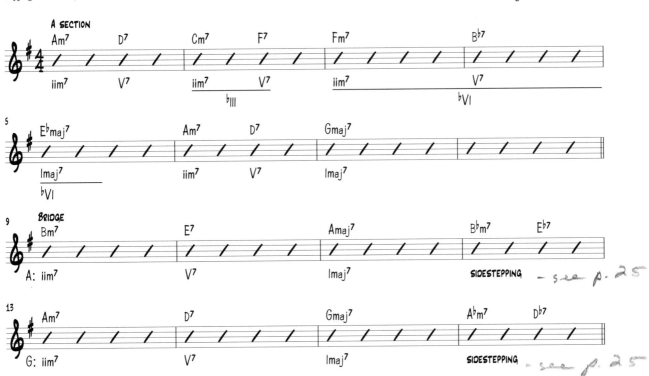

– see p. 25

– see p. 25

The A section begins with a simple iim^7–V^7, inserts a brief iim^7–V^7 of $\flat$III, and then an extended move and resolution to $\flat$VI, before returning to the home key of G. The bridge modulates to A, and then returns to G. Brief ii–V^7s at the end of each four-bar half of the bridge are embellishing, not structural. They chromatically move into the upcoming chords using alternate functions of the dominant chord (see below).

Dominant chords do not always act as V^7 chords. There are other possibilities.

Blues Dominant Sevenths

In the blues, tonic and subdominant chords are more likely to receive a ♭7 than they are a natural seventh or natural sixth. Although this chord will look exactly like a dominant chord, it will not function as one unless it's in the right structural place to do that. Let's consider a typical jazz blues:

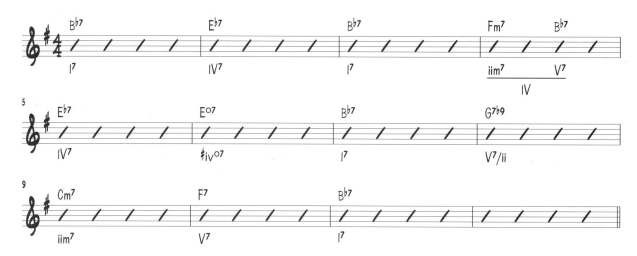

The B♭7 in measure 1 receives an A♭, not because it is a V7 chord, but because the blues sound calls for a ♭7. Doesn't the blues sound also call for a ♭3? No. There's a vast difference in how the blues treats these two notes. We've all heard great blues singers bend or "worry" the third of the scale, so that you can't really tell if it's a natural third or a flat. The point is, they are both permissible notes in the blues sound. Ever heard a singer do that with the seventh? No, they won't. If they bend the ♭7 it will be downward, toward the sixth. The point is, the default seventh chord in the blues is the dominant seventh. That's true for both I and IV. But when needed, the dominant seventh in the blues can take on its V7 role as well. We see that in bars 4, 8, and 10.

It is helpful to distinguish dominant chords that have functions other than V7 because the distinction will influence our choice of upper structures. Generally, ♭9 or ♭13 will not work on a blues dominant, since they imply too much of a tendency toward resolution. But 9 and 13 are perfectly acceptable. ♯11 can be used, but it is very dissonant. ♯9, which is normally quite dissonant on a V7, is an excellent choice for I7 in the blues, since it hits the flatted third. But it is *not* a normal choice on the IV7, since the resulting pitch is far removed from the key. Here are suggested upper structures for blues dominant sevenths:

I7   9, 13, ♯9, ♯11 (very dissonant)

IV7   9, 13, ♯11

Tritone Substitutions

The strongest root motion is by fourth/fifth or stepwise. Chords moving by thirds do not have the same energy. That's what makes the ii–V^7 progression so powerful— the roots move up a fourth and down a fifth (or down a fifth and up a fourth). There is also a pre-dominant/dominant/tonic progression that consists entirely of stepwise motion.

keep in mind for my chord voicings

Consider the notes in a G$^{7\flat5}$ chord, G, B, D$\flat$, and F. If these notes are rearranged with D$\flat$ on the bottom, the chord becomes D$\flat$, F, G, and B, which is an enharmonic spelling of a D$\flat^{7\flat5}$. Any V$^{7\flat5}$ chord is a rearrangement of the notes of a dominant seventh a tritone away. Within the key, we may say that V$^{7\flat5}$ = $\flat$II$^{7\flat5}$. This is known as a tritone substitution or a substitute dominant. Since the fifth of a chord is often omitted and a $\sharp$11 is an option on a V7 chord anyway, this relationship holds for all dominant sevenths. *Any dominant seventh chord can be replaced by the dominant seventh a tritone away*, regardless of the quality of the fifth or upper structures. This is known as tritone substitution. In analysis, the chord is indicated either as subV^7 or $\flat$II^7. Another handy thing to know about tritone subs is that the 9 and 13 of one dominant seventh become the $\flat$13 and $\sharp$9 of the other dominant, respectively.

*D tritone = Ab or A is tritone sub G = Db
Ab = D tritone sub D*

Other Dominant Chord Functions

Another class of dominant chord function, much less common than the tritone substitution, involves stepwise resolution upward. This one is actually sanctioned by hundreds of years of practice. In classical music, going all the way back to the baroque period, a V chord would sometimes go to vi (in major) or $\flat$VI (in minor) as a *deceptive cadence*. The theoretical justification is that vi (or $\flat$VI) is a substitute for the tonic chord. But the actual result is stepwise resolution upward. *For our purposes, a V^7 chord can resolve upward by half or whole step.*

Now the passing chords in the bridge to "Lazy Bird" can be explained. The E$\flat^7$ anticipates the approaching D^7 as a tritone substitution. The D$\flat^7$ anticipates an approaching D^7 from a half step below.

*b/c Ab would contain b/c Abm7 Eb7? Bbm7 Eb7?
b/c back to the A section's Am7 D7*

Final Thoughts on Analysis

Analysis is a valuable tool for anyone who wants to get the most from a real book. It can help you identify the crucial chords, choose upper structures, and construct appropriate bass motion. Additionally, it can help you understand a tune as a complete entity and see how it's put together and how it works. It's much better to really know a song this way than to just memorize a string of chords.

It's not important that your way of looking at a chord progression be the same as someone else's. Analysis need not be definitive or accepted by everyone in order to work for you. For example, as a young musician I had trouble remembering the chords to "The Girl from Ipanema" in various keys. They didn't make sense to me, until one day I worked out an analysis that made the bridge click for me. Here it is:

THE GIRL FROM IPANEMA
(GARÔTA DE IPANEMA)

Music by Antonio Carlos Jobim
English Words by Norman Gimbel
Original Words by Vinicius de Moraes

The bridge really involves only two functions, followed by a turnaround. It begins by modulating up a half step with a Imaj⁷–IV⁷ progression. Then the same thing up a minor third. Then the same thing a half step higher, which is the key of the subdominant. A common turnaround sends you to the home key. What could be simpler?

There may be other ways to view this bridge, but the trick is to link chords together so you can see the big picture, whatever that looks like to you. That way you get to know a tune thoroughly and mastery in various keys is attainable.

— CHAPTER 3 —
FORM

Take what I learned in previous chapter and conduct harmonic analysis of these tunes in Chapter 3.

"I like to play things that people understand, or maybe tunes that they could recognize. And so—I play for the people, just as much as for myself." – Ben Webster

"The more constraints one imposes, the more one frees one's self."
– Igor Stravinsky

Standard Popular Song Forms

Very few pieces of music continue with new material from start to finish. Instead, composers have discovered that repeating sections of a composition allows the listener to understand and remember the music better. In between these repeated sections will be contrasting sections of different material.

Classical compositions often have very elaborate forms with prescribed sections and modulations. But popular songs generally fall into a few basic patterns that can be explained by simply noting the individual sections and their repeats. We give them letter names (A, B, and so forth), and indicate a repeat or recurrence of that section by showing the same letter. AA means the first section repeats. ABA Means that the A section is heard again after a contrasting section. Instead of its letter name, a single contrasting section is commonly referred to as the bridge.

The form of a jazz or standard tune can be almost anything, but there are a few basic models that dominate the repertoire. Let's have a look at a typical standard tune, Hoagy Carmichael's "Georgia on My Mind" (1930). Its structure is representative of many thousands of tunes of its kind:

GEORGIA ON MY MIND

Words by Stuart Gorrell
Music by Hoagy Carmichael

The song is 32 bars long and will of course be repeated several times in performance (thus the chords in parentheses at the end—they are to be omitted the very last time). The song divides evenly into four sections of eight measures each. The first two and last sections are very similar, while the third section (the bridge) contrasts, with changes in harmony, melodic shape, and rhythm. Here is the form of the tune:

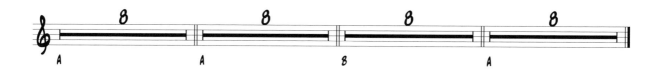

With some tunes there are substantial differences between the A sections, but not enough to give them a different letter name. In that case, we could call a slightly contrasting section A', and the other A" if necessary. Such detail is not usually required. The important thing is to get an overall grasp of the form.

Sometimes a tune will have a built-in "tag" or extension at the end, lengthening the form by some even number of measures. "I Remember You" has a four-measure tag. But the form is still AABA (or, AABA', to be exact).

I REMEMBER YOU

Words by Johnny Mercer
Music by Victor Schertzinger

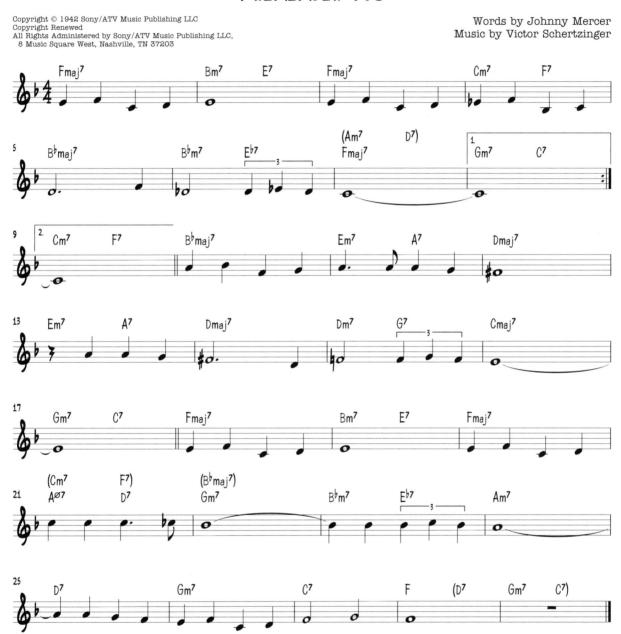

Another common song form is ABAC. (In truth, most ABAC tunes are really ABAB', but they are seldom referred to that way.) Frank Loesser's "If I Were A Bell" follows this pattern.

IF I WERE A BELL

By Frank Loesser

Here is a diagram of the form:

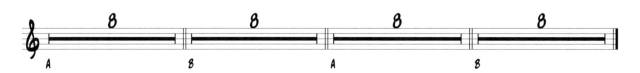

The 12-bar blues is another very common formal structure. It is important to realize that not every blues song is 12 bars long, but most of them are. (When W.C. Handy was attempting to get his "St. Louis Blues" published—one of the most famous blues songs in history—several publishers commented that the 12-bar choruses each had four measures missing!) In the early years of the 20th century, blues referred more to a feeling than a form. But in time, more and more blues compositions began to adopt the 12-bar pattern. Unlike other song forms, where the harmony can be almost anything, the 12-bar blues follows a common basic chord structure. Almost every 12-bar blues is a variation or adaptation of this pattern:

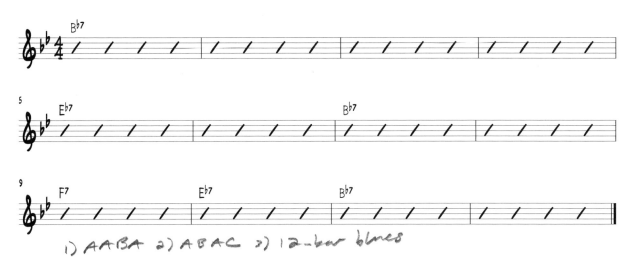

1) AABA 2) ABAC 3) 12-bar blues

These three forms go a long way in covering a great number of songs in the popular and jazz literature, but many more are possible. Some simple variations of these include, "Gee Baby Ain't I Good to You" (a 16-bar tune in AABA form), and "That Old Black Magic" (in AABA form, extending some 64 measures with tag for a total of 72 measures). There are also tunes in ABC form, AB form, and simply through-composed—that is, with no repeating sections.

Harmonic Templates

Analyze and be able to improv over these

As any psychologist will tell you, the best way to grasp new information is to tie it to old information. That is, we learn things by relating them to things we already know. In more than 100 years of composing, songwriters in a variety of fields have presented us with a staggering number of tunes. When you consider that some major songwriters published more than a thousand songs, and that thousands of people have had songs published, we're dealing with astronomical numbers.

Fortunately for us, they were not reinventing the wheel every time they wrote a song. Most songs contain tried-and-true chord progressions that occur in hundreds of other songs. Some songs actually contain the exact same chord progressions. (Chords are not protected by copyright law.) For anyone who has already learned several songs in a specific genre, it is almost impossible not to find familiar patterns when a new song is encountered.

The intention of this section is to expand upon this concept. Beyond the blues, there are many other templates—some covering entire tunes and some only a few measures—that can rein in hundreds of tunes and make order out of chaos. It would be well to learn these songs in several keys. Although learning songs and exercises in every key is a noble and lofty goal, it's not always the best use of one's time. Learning each of these progressions in three or four common keys should do the trick. The goal is that whenever you see or hear a new tune, you can relate to another tune, or a combination of tunes.

The Blues. While the outline above shows basic blues harmony, and is really all you need for some songs, most jazz tunes add many more chords than shown above. Two sets of blues changes are shown below. The first adds some ii–Vs and passing chords to add more of a jazz sound to the progression. The second adds several more ii–Vs, and tends to move away from the basic blues sound. These are often called "John Lewis Blues" or "Blues for Alice" Changes, named after the Charlie Parker tune.

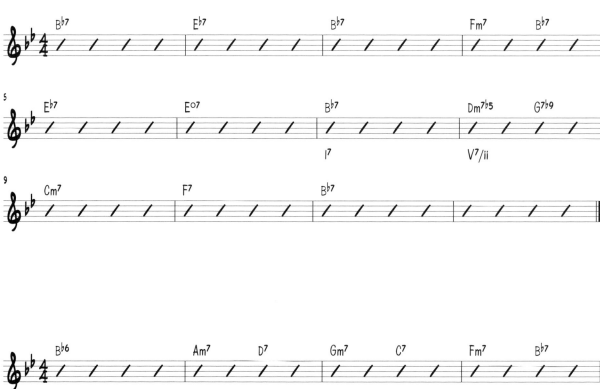

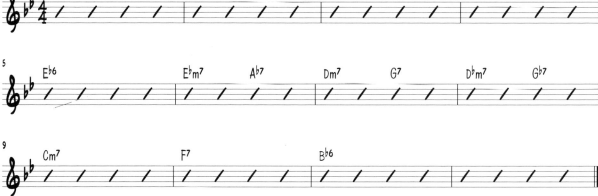

Minor Blues. Although not nearly as common as major blues, a substantial number of blues songs are in a minor key. Here is the barebones structure for a minor blues. The I and IV chords simply become minor, with supporting ii and V7 chords altered accordingly:

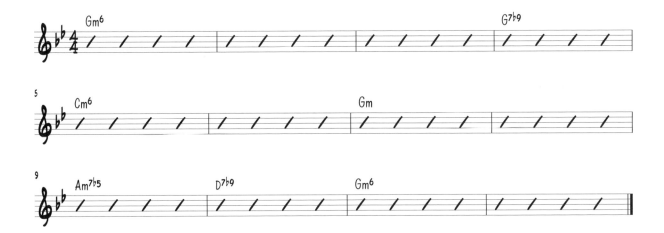

Rhythm Changes. The name derives from George Gershwin's song "I Got Rhythm" (1930). No one knows for sure why these chords are named after this tune, since the harmonic sequence was around before Gershwin wrote his tune, and "I Got Rhythm" doesn't strictly adhere to the Rhythm Changes model, since it has a four-bar tag! Nevertheless, the name stuck, and, next to the blues, Rhythm Changes are the most important structure in jazz.

Below is a basic version of Rhythm Changes. Dozens of frequently played tunes follow a harmonic structure that is related to this, and countless variations are possible. The important thing is to recognize when a tune is built on Rhythm Changes, or something like Rhythm Changes. If you had to describe the structure in words, you might say, "An AABA song that hovers around the tonic for four measures, then goes to IV, via V⁷/IV, and then back to the tonic. Chords come every two beats in the A section. The B section (bridge) follows a Circle of Fifths, starting with a dominant seventh built on the third note of the key. Chords come every two measures.

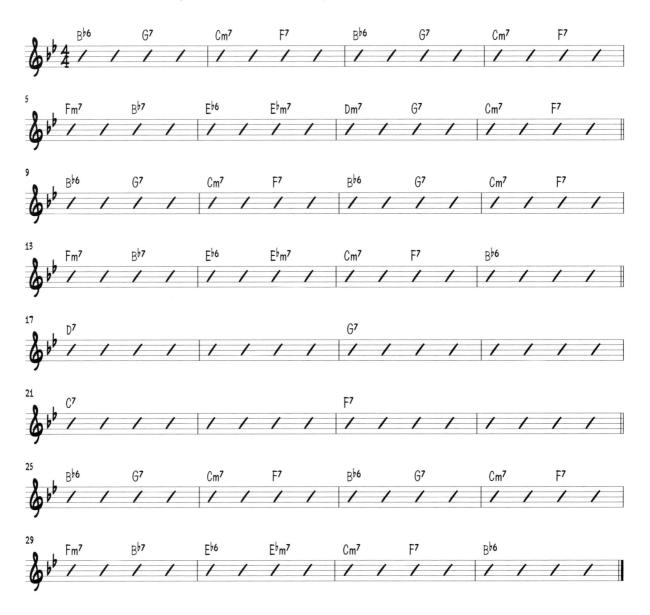

Honeysuckle Changes. Fats Waller's "Honeysuckle Rose" was once close behind Rhythm Changes as a very common jam tune. Many tunes share the opening chord structure, the Honeysuckle Bridge, or both.

Long Rhythm Changes. Some tunes incorporate an opening section that resembles Rhythm Changes, except that the first four chords are spread out over a measure each. The first eight measures look like this:

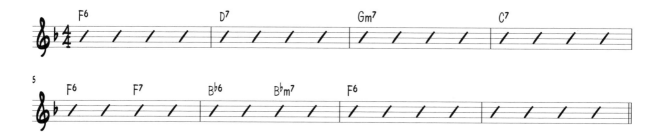

Doxy Changes. The Sonny Rollins tune "Doxy" is well known as a favorite set of "blowing changes" (that is, chord sequences that are favorites at jam sessions). Although only 16 measures long, the tune follows standard AABA form. Several tunes follow a basic structural pattern related to this one, including the Dixieland standards "Jada," and "How Come You Do Me?" as well as Horace Silver's classic "The Preacher."

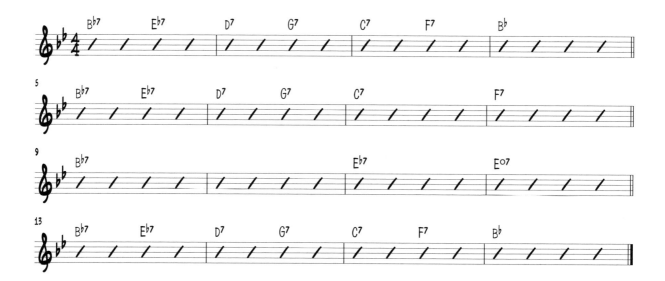

Indiana Changes. The old jazz standard "Indiana (Back Home Again in Indiana)" furnished the chord structure for the Miles Davis tune "Donna Lee," a bebop standard. As with all these templates, the precise chords to either the original or derivative tunes would probably vary from this template somewhat, but these changes clearly show the overall harmonic structure.

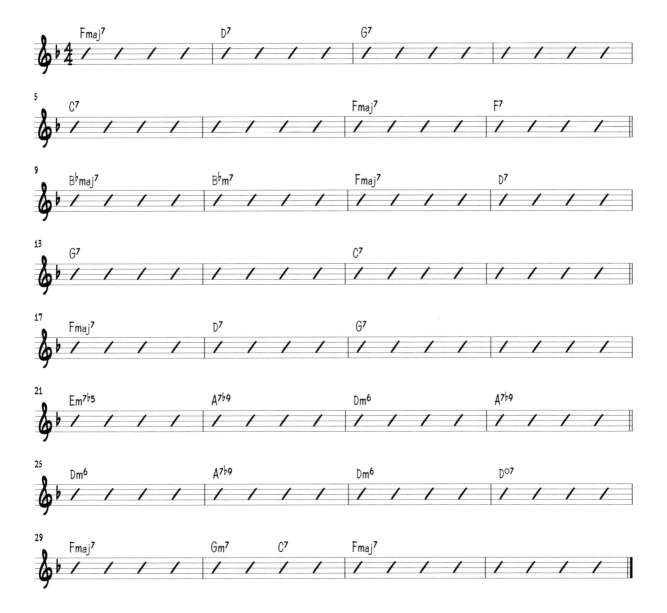

Rose Room Changes. Although Duke Ellington's tune "In a Mellow Tone" on the same changes (and in the same key) is better known, "Rose Room" came first, and was a favorite blowing tune of swing musicians. The ABAB tune hits a number of common progressions, including the opening V^7/V–V^7–I.

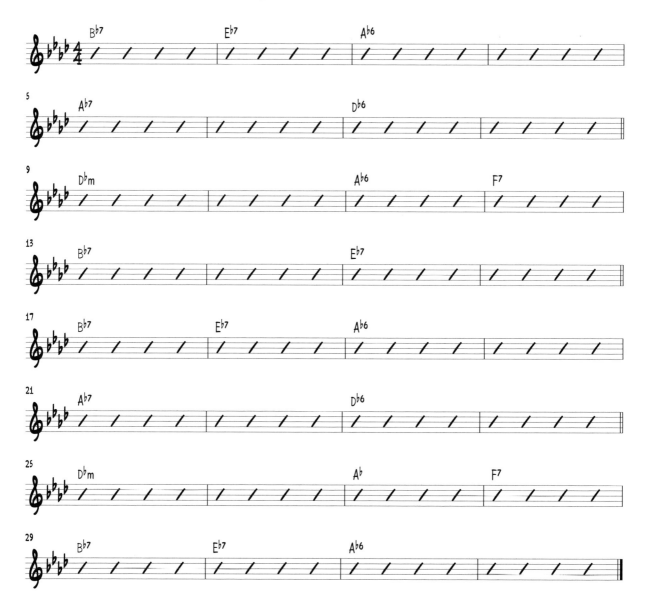

Pick Yourself Up Changes. Dating from the mid-1930s, Jerome Kern's "Pick Yourself Up" is one of the earlier tunes noted for its fast-moving ii–V⁷ progressions, going through several keys. There are many bebop tunes that incorporate similar patterns.

Miss Jones Bridge. Richard Rodgers's "Have You Met Miss Jones?" has one of the most famous bridges in the literature. This chord sequence predates Coltrane Changes and most likely helped inspire them. The tune modulates to B♭ in measure 17, and then flirts with the keys both a major third lower and major third higher before returning to the tonic. Here is the bridge:

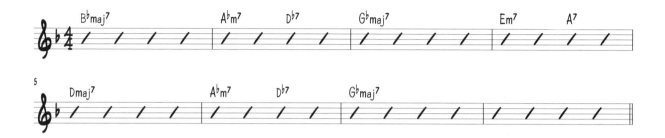

While many more harmonic templates can be found, those listed above will go a long way in explaining progressions found in hundreds of tunes. The idea is that when encountering a new song, you won't have to learn it from scratch.

— CHAPTER 4 —
PLAYING THE FORM

"The bandstand is a sacred place." – **Wynton Marsalis**

"If you don't make mistakes, you aren't really trying." – **Coleman Hawkins**

The Arrangement — *study these + listen to them for*
@ the same time

Most songs, whether jazz, pop, or whatever genre, are relatively short, providing
less than a minute of music. The general procedure is then to repeat the song one *sonic*
or several times, varying the song in some way, until a suitable length is reached. *architect*
In jazz, that means playing a chorus rather strictly, so the melody can be heard, *ideas.*
improvising on the form several times, and repeating the melody for the last chorus.

Within this conceptual framework, countless variations are possible. These historic
recordings will give some idea of the tremendous freedom bands have in putting
together an unwritten arrangement.

"Scrapple from the Apple" – Charlie Parker & Miles Davis, 4 November 1947

8 bars	introduction
Chorus 1	horns play melody, alto improvises bridge
Chorus 2	alto solo
Chorus 3	trumpet solo
Chorus 4	piano first half, bass bridge, horns play melody out
8 bars	ending

"Robin's Nest" – Johnny Griffin and Eddie "Lockjaw" Davis, *Live at Minton's,*
1 January 1961

4 bars	introduction
Chorus 1	tenors play melody
Choruses 2–4	lockjaw solo
Choruses 5–7	piano solo
Choruses 8–10	griffin solo
Chorus 11	tenors play riff figure for 16 bars, bass solo 8 bars, tenors play melody last 8 bars
2 bars	ending

"Have You Met Miss Jones?" – Stan Getz and Bob Brookmeyer, 16 April 1953

4 bars	introduction
Chorus 1	tenor plays melody, trombone takes bridge, tenor takes two-bar break at the end
Chorus 2	tenor solo
Chorus 3	trombone solo
Chorus 4	piano solo
Chorus 5	horns trade fours with drums, tenor takes bridge, last 8 both horns
4 bars	ending

"Lazy Bird" – John Coltrane *Blue Train*, 15 September 1957

8 bars	intro
Chorus 1	trumpet plays melody
Choruses 2–3	trumpet solo
Choruses 4–5	trombone solo
Choruses 6–8	tenor solo
Choruses 9–10	piano solo
Chorus 11	bass solo
Chorus 12	drum solo
Chorus 13	trumpet plays melody
4 bars (+ holds)	ending

"There Will Never Be Another You" – *Wes Montgomery with the Billy Taylor Trio, November 1963*

Chorus 1	guitar plays melody
Chorus 2	piano solo
Chorus 3	guitar solo
Chorus 4	piano and guitar trade fours
Chorus 5	piano plays melody with ritardando and ending

"There Is No Greater Love" – Sonny Stitt and Gene Ammons, 27 August 1961

8 bars	introduction
Chorus 1	Stitt melody first 8, Ammons 9–15, Stitt bridge, Ammons last 8 with two-bar break
Chorus 2	Ammons solo
Chorus 3-4	Stitt solo
Chorus 5	Stitt melody first 8, Ammons 9–15, bridge together, Stitt last 8
44 bars (!)	repeated tag ending, Stitt and Ammons trading

"Oleo" – Miles Davis & Hank Mobley, *In Person Friday Night at the Blackhawk*, 21 April 1961

Chorus 1	trumpet plays melody first 8, horns together second 8, piano bridge, horns last 8
Choruses 2–5	trumpet
Choruses 6–14	tenor
Choruses 15–16	piano
Chorus 17	horns play melody, bridge rhythm section only

"Georgia on My Mind" – Shirley Horn, 21 September 1993 (release date)

8 bars	Shirley sings bridge for intro
Chorus	Shirley sings one chorus

"I Got It Bad" – Bill Evans, 18 September 1956

Chorus 1	solo piano rubato
Chorus 2	repeats back to bridge, solo continues

Turnarounds

Whatever form the song takes, it is likely to be played more than once. That means that the final measures must do more than just sit on the tonic chord. They must "turn the tune around" and send it back to the top. The chords that do this might be indicated in the music and they might not. Even if they are, you don't have to observe those exact chords. There are many possibilities.

The most common turnarounds consist of four chords of two beats each spanning two measures. The function is to set up the top of the tune or the next section of the tune. They can also serve as introductions. There are no rules to turnarounds, other than maintaining the character of the piece and insuring a smooth transition to the next section. Here are some turnarounds in F:

F^6	Dm^7	Gm^7	C^7
$Fmaj^7$	D^7	Gm^7	C^7
F^6	D^7	G^7	C^7
Am^7	D^7	Gm^7	C^7
$Fmaj^7$	$F\sharp^{o7}$	Gm^7	C^7
$Fmaj^7$	$A\flat^{o7}$	Gm^7	C^7
Am^7	$A\flat m^7$	Gm^7	C^7
$Fmaj^7$	$A\flat^7$	G^7	C^7
F^6	D^7	$D\flat^7$	C^7
F^6	D^7	G^7	$G\flat^7$
F^6	$A\flat^7$	G^7	$G\flat^7$

Dozens more like this are possible, without introducing any radical harmonic departures. And these examples don't even consider the variations in color that can be achieved with upper structures.

Introductions

Just like books, songs often have introductions. And, just like in a book, a song's introduction is meant to tell you what's coming, build up anticipation, and set a mood. As a practical consideration, it also gives the musicians in the band time to get ready to play the tune.

An introduction consists of a few measures of music in front of the song. It can be taken from the song or it can be original. It can be in tempo or rubato (out of meter). It can be improvised or worked out in advance. There really are no guidelines as to what it should be. Anything is possible, and anything and everything has been tried. The pianist can play the intro alone, the entire rhythm section can play it, or the horns can join in. A horn can play alone, as can the bass, or even drums (very effective on fast tunes). It can be four measures, eight measures, two measures, one measure, an odd number of measures, or a whole chorus. So the plan here is to lay out some possibilities, starting with the simplest (which are often the best), and give you an idea how you might come up with your own intros.

No introduction. A perfectly viable option is to have no introduction at all. There's nothing wrong with starting right in with a song. This is particularly effective with songs that have long pickups, such as Duke Ellington's "In a Sentimental Mood":

IN A SENTIMENTAL MOOD

By Duke Ellington

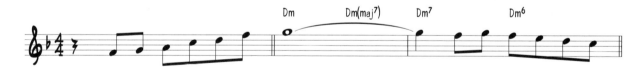

Chord or arpeggio introduction. This usually applies to ballads. The pianist or guitarist will play one (or more) chords out of tempo prior to the downbeat.

Verse as introduction. A song's verse can serve as the introduction. Verses are particularly effective in vocal performance. They can be played either in time or rubato, but they are equally suited to instrumental performance. Increasingly, real books have been including verses for standard songs. They serve very well as a song's built-in introduction.

Four-measure introductions. Four-bar intros are the most common. They usually rely on an improvised or prepared melody, since four measures are not really enough of the tune to quote for good effect. Often the pianist will set up some kind of turnaround and provide a melody to it.

Here is a generic intro to a tune in F. The turnaround is repeated with slight variations in chords and melody. If the band weren't ready to come in at the end of this, it could be repeated, either verbatim or with modifications. Thus, a four-measure introduction could easily be adapted to an eight-measure introduction, twelve measures, or any multiple of four.

At faster tempos, you might just want to improvise a line over the changes:

Eight-measure introductions. The last eight measures of the song can serve as the introduction. This can be done either in tempo (for medium or up-tempo tunes) or freely (for ballads). Eight-measure intros are particularly effective when the first chorus is going to be sung, but they also work in instrumental contexts. Just start eight measures from the end and place the turnaround in the final measures, just as you would between choruses.

If the tune is slow, the final measure might sound a bit stagnant. In other words, if a song ends on a whole note, or a whole note followed by a whole rest, that's not very active set-up to the top of the tune. One remedy is to shorten the last eight bars. In other words, start eight measures from the end, but after six measures jump directly to the top of the tune. On his 1957 album *Blue Trane*, John Coltrane plays the last section of "I'm Old Fashioned" out of meter, accompanied only by piano, as the introduction. Then, two measures from the end, the meter starts and he jumps directly to the top of the tune.

I'M OLD FASHIONED

Words by Johnny Mercer
Music by Jerome Kern

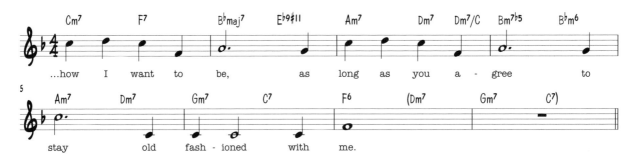

Two measures from end …

… jump directly to top of tune

Some tunes work better if two or more measures from the end of the tune are repeated instead of starting eight from the end. Here is an intro to "There Will Never Be Another You." Bars 3 and 4 from the end are played three times before going into the last two bars.

THERE WILL NEVER BE ANOTHER YOU

Lyric by Mack Gordon
Music by Harry Warren

This approach also works when the third and fourth bars from the end contain a particularly interesting melody. Here is an intro to "Robbin's Nest." As you can see, the notes of the melody may have to be modified somewhat to accommodate the repeat.

ROBBIN'S NEST

By Sir Charles Thompson
and Illinois Jacquet

The strategy of stretching the last four bars to eight also makes a very effective ending. Any tune that is suited for this kind of intro is also suited for a similar ending.

If an eight-measure intro is improvised, as opposed to being taken from the last eight measures of the tune, then the rhythm section is not confined to chords every two beats. Here is a "long" turnaround to the key of Cminor, consisting of a string of ii–Vs in minor keys:

Now what if the first chord of the song is not the tonic? It usually doesn't matter. If a song starts with a typical iim⁷–V⁷ progression, you don't really need to set up the iim⁷ chord, since there is nothing wrong with a V⁷ chord being followed by a iim⁷ chord. Here's an example. The final ii–V⁷ of the intro (measure 4) is followed by another ii–V⁷ at the start of the tune (measures 5–6).

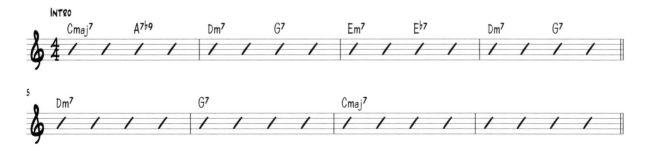

Another possibility is to set up that Dm⁷ in bar 1 by placing V^7/ii in front of it:

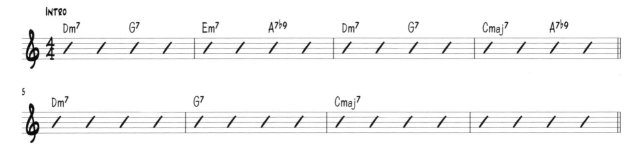

Pedal point introductions. Many introductions use pedal point. Simply hold the fifth of the tonic chord in the bass, usually with a repeated off-beat rhythm, and add some sort of stagnant or repeating figure on top. This kind of intro is usually eight measures long.

Because the harmony is static, just about any chords or notes that contribute to the "floating" quality will work. For example, borrowing a couple of chords from the minor we come up with this:

I've indicated two empty measures at the end for a regular turnaround to set up the tune—but this is not a rule. The pedal effect can just as easily go to the very end of the intro.

Introductions to Latin tunes. Latin tunes need special treatment. Traditionally, Latin music is more about rhythm and mood than about functional chord progression. Vamps often work well for introductions to Latin tunes, as they allow time for establishing a rhythmic groove and setting a mood. Latin intros are often harmonically static, and can repeat for some length of time before the tune begins. Sus chords, chords containing the 11th, triads with an added ninth, and repeating, nonfunctional chord progressions are often used.

For example, a tune in G minor might begin as follows:

For two-chord Latin intros, alternating Imaj^7 with $\flat$IImaj^7 is common:

As is Imaj^7 with $\flat$VIImaj^7:

Vamping on a ii–V^7 progression can also be effective, especially on fast tunes:

If the tune happens to start on a ii chord, simply resolve the progression to the tonic in the second half of the intro:

49

If the chord structure of the tune is functional in a traditional way, as will be the case when you perform a standard as a Latin tune, then a common turnaround will work. However, it is probably best to slow the harmonic rhythm by having only one chord per measure:

Endings

Just as there are infinite possibilities for starting a tune, so are there countless possibilities for ending it. The most obvious is, just stop. Seriously, on fast jazz tunes—e.g., "Donna Lee," "Oleo," "It Don't Mean A Thing," and so many others—there is nothing more effective than the whole band just stopping abruptly on a dime. No ritardando, no hold, just an immediate halt after the last note. Here are the last four measures of Sonny Rollins's "Oleo":

OLEO

By Sonny Rollins

If the last note of a fast tune is a long note, then a hold is more effective, as with the ending of John Coltrane's "Giant Steps":

GIANT STEPS

By John Coltrane

When holding the last note of a tune, whether a jazz standard or pop tune, it is customary (though not required) for the soloist to improvise freely on the last chord.

If the tune is of a more moderate tempo, a slight slowing of the last couple of measures is usually necessary. Here are the last four measures of Weill's "My Ship":

MY SHIP

Words by Ira Gershwin
Music by Kurt Weill

If the tune is slow enough, this kind of ending might have an unaccompanied cadenza inserted. After the ritardando on the fourth and third bars from the end, the tempo will stop and the soloist will improvise a cadenza of unspecified duration prior to the last chord. It can be as little as a couple of arpeggios or as much as a half-a-minute or more of noodling. Then, usually on the soloists cue, everyone comes in on the last chord.

For medium to moderately fast tunes, the tag ending is one of the most used. The formula is simple: The last two measures of the song are replaced by a iim⁷–V⁷/ii progression, after which the song resumes four measures from the end. During the added two measures, the melody is either freely improvised or consists of some modification of the third and fourth bars from the end.

Here is a tag ending on "There Is No Greater Love":

THERE IS NO GREATER LOVE

Words by Marty Symes
Music by Isham Jones

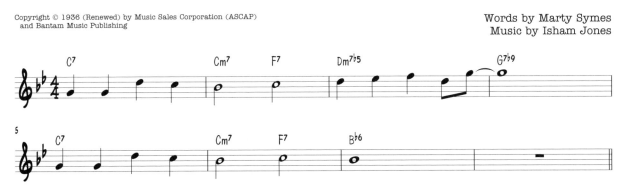

Of course, you will still need to figure out some kind of ending for the last chord, but the tag signals that the end is coming and helps to break the momentum. For example, if this tune were played at a bright tempo, simply putting a hold on the last note probably wouldn't work. It would be too abrupt. But after tagging the tune, that's all you would need.

A tag need not be just one time. After cycling back to four measures from the end, you can tag the tune all over again. This can be done numerous times. Players like Sonny Stitt were known for tagging a tune dozens of times, freely improvising over the cycled chord changes.

On some tunes, it works better to repeat the third and fourth measures from the end verbatim. Then you would play those measures a third time, and on to the last two measures, making four additional bars total. Refer back to the example giving the last eight measures of "There Will Never Be Another You" as an intro (page 46). It works equally well as an ending.

What if a tune already has a built-in tag? In that case, a traditional tag probably isn't appropriate, since it would sound repetitious. A solution that sometimes works (harmony permitting) is to tag bars 3 and 4 from the end, not up a whole step, but up a minor third. Here is the ending to "I Remember You," starting eight bars from the end, since the first tag is part of the song. After the Gm⁷ to C⁷ in the second system below, we should go directly to an F chord, but instead we take the harmony up a minor third. A very good strategy when it fits.

I REMEMBER YOU

Words by Johnny Mercer
Music by Victor Schertzinger

Breaks

The break has a long-sanctioned history in jazz, and was at one time the only part of a song that was improvised. (Listen to the Louis Armstrong/Joe Oliver recordings as an example of this.) All instruments stop playing except one, but the tempo doesn't stop. A break is generally two or four measures long, but both shorter and longer breaks have been used. A common and effective use of the break is for the band to stop for the last two measures of the first chorus, allowing the first soloist to improvise two measures unaccompanied prior to the top of his chorus. The soloist is then free to improvise not only the line, but a harmonic turnaround of his or her choice. This is how the end of the first chorus of "There Is No Greater Love" would appear with a two-bar break:

While this is the most common place, breaks can be inserted in other places as well. They are a very important part of traditional jazz and are sometimes built into the melody of the tune at various places.

Trading

Trading refers to alternating four measures of improvisation between different instruments. While fours are the most common, it is also possible to trade eights, twos, or other numbers of measures. One way is for two horn players to go back and forth with each other. Another is for a horn player to alternate with the drummer. If there is more than one horn player, then they will take turns alternating with the drummer, and perhaps include the piano and guitar in the routine. In recent years, trading eights with the drummer has become increasingly common because it allows the player to develop more advanced ideas.

Interpreting the Melody

If a tune in a real book is notated as a jazz tune, it can often be played exactly as written, in terms of notes and rhythm. All you need to do is know how to swing and articulate in the appropriate style. "Oleo" is an example of such a tune. All the rhythms are already indicated:

OLEO

By Sonny Rollins

Latin tunes should also generally be played exactly as written. Many contain rhythmic intricacies that are very much a part of the character of the tune and mesh carefully with the words. Here is the opening to "Triste." Although it would be easy enough to juggle the syncopations and come up with something else, it is better to defer to Jobim, who was a master of rhythmic nuance.

TRISTE

By Antonio Carlos Jobim

Sad__ is to live in sol - i - tude,_____

But many of the tunes found in real books are not jazz originals—they are standard songs from the Great American Songbook, written for the stage, movies, or home performance. They were not intended as jazz songs (many were written before jazz was known to the general public), and were not written as such. "Play it the way the composer wrote it" is often poor advice for the jazz musician.

On the other hand, you don't want to destroy a beautiful melody by overdoing it. Many songs commonly found in real books were written by the greatest masters of melodic invention ever known to American music—Jerome Kern, George Gershwin, Richard Rogers, Harold Arlen, Cole Porter, Irving Berlin, and many others. When interpreting their music, it is always important to remember that they knew exactly what they were about—they were simply writing for a different type of performance. Changes in their melodies and rhythms must be made, but they must be made judiciously. The jazz greats were absolute masters at this. Among the many recorded examples of expert and artistic interpretation of standard songs, I would recommend Charlie Parker's recordings with strings and John Coltrane's Prestige recordings.

Below is the melody to "There Is No Greater Love," with the melody (not necessarily verbatim from the sheet music, but as it might be found in a real book) on the bottom and a possible interpretation on top. In keeping with jazz interpretation from its very beginnings, the crucial element is to add syncopation and rhythmic variety. Notice that the contour and basic notes of the melody remain intact.

THERE IS NO GREATER LOVE

Words by Marty Symes
Music by Isham Jones

The example below in the same format shows an interpretation of "I Hear a Rhapsody." Without getting too fussy with articulations (and it is impossible to show jazz articulation exactly), I have shown that all quarter notes are not necessarily played the same way. Notice that when notes are added, the intention is to embellish the melody, not replace it.

I HEAR A RHAPSODY

By George Frajos,
Jack Baker and Dick Gasparre

Even if it were possible to do so, I don't think specific rules should be given for interpreting or embellishing a melody. There are too many variables, including the temperament and mood of the performer. One thing to keep in mind, however, is that we are depending on the listener's knowledge of the song and expectations of what is to come next. Therefore, a simpler, well-known song (say, "Bye Bye Blackbird") will tolerate a greater degree of manipulation since everybody knows it and it's not very complicated. Tunes on the other end of that spectrum (say, "Pick Yourself Up" or "My Ship") invite a stricter reading of the tune.

— CHAPTER 5 —
BASS LINES

"I just play any go-to-hell note, as long as it swings." — **Pops Foster**

"There is no such thing as wrong notes. It's what you do after." — **Art Tatum**

A bass line is a continuous series of notes in the lower register that outlines the harmony while providing a rhythmic pulse. It may consist of half or quarter notes, or it may contain more complex rhythms. A "walking" bass line usually refers to a regular stream of quarter notes. However, with bass lines of all types, it is usually good practice to "break" the pattern occasionally to avoid a "motor rhythm" effect.

Bass lines are very powerful entities in driving the harmony and the rhythm. They are, of course, a bass player's stock-in-trade, but other musicians need to know how to construct bass lines as well. Pianists and guitarists often employ bass lines in solo performance. Any musician who plays with a bass player will profit from knowing exactly how the bass player communicates through the bass line. And there is no better way for getting a feel for a song when reading from a real book at the keyboard than to lay down a bass line in the left hand.

Bass Lines in Two

The simplest bass lines are in two, and this is a technique that's not to be overlooked. It is very effective on ballads and medium slow tempos, and was the preferred bass line in the early years of jazz. When chords come every two beats there are few choices to make—just play the roots. When chords last for the full measure, the root followed by the fifth usually works. For variety, half-notes can occasionally be replaced by quarter notes going to other chord tones.

Here is the opening to Jerome Kern's "I'm Old Fashioned," starting simply, and then adding some quarter notes:

I'M OLD FASHIONED

Words by Johnny Mercer
Music by Jerome Kern

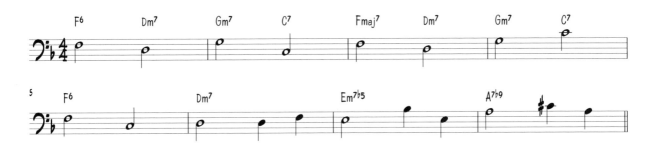

Sometimes it is better to begin with the fifth of the chord. This may be done to avoid a repeated note:

A measure starting on the fifth may also be used simply to add variety. This is shown below in a two-beat bass line on "I Got It Bad and That Ain't Good." Notice how the line is improved by reversing the root-fifth pattern in the second measure. Also, note how in measure 5 the bass note repeats. This sets up contrast, and avoids repeating the E, with the measure that follows:

I GOT IT BAD AND THAT AIN'T GOOD

Words by Paul Francis Webster
Music by Duke Ellington

Sometimes, when playing in two, you may wish to simplify chords in order to clarify the harmonic progression. This is particularly true for bridges and other passages that may stray far from the original harmonic area. The bridge to "Have You Met Miss Jones?" is such a tune. In the suggested bass line below, I've chosen to remove the related iim⁷ chords, leaving just the dominants (which is what Rodgers originally wrote). Although each measure now has repeated notes, the harmonic progression itself is interesting and busy enough, so that it remains an effective bass line.

HAVE YOU MET MISS JONES?

Words by Lorenz Hart
Music by Richard Rodgers

As a general rule, when playing in two, repeated notes within the measure are preferable to repeated notes across the bar line. This is true because, when the chord changes, we want to hear that change reflected in the bass line.

Bass Lines in Four

At first, it might seem that simply playing up and down the chord would yield a basic acceptable bass line, but that is not the case. While bass players may do this for specific styles (say, boogie woogie), or for contrast or special effect, playing all chord tones is not a staple of bass line construction.

One approach to playing in four is simply to play in two but repeat every note. Some bass players refer to this approach as a "walking two-beat" or just "walking two." This is the classic bass technique of the big band era. They did this for two reasons: (1) They were playing dance music, driving a big band, and had little, if any, amplification. They needed to lay down the beat and be heard. More complicated bass lines would not be nearly as powerful in this context. (2) The repeated notes of the bass are very effective in tunes that employ recurring patterns or riffs. To demonstrate this, here is the melody of "Opus One," along with a suggested bass line. Notice how the repeated notes of the bass line complement the riff figure. Also notice that, as with any good bass line, the pattern is broken occasionally (measures 4 and 6).

OPUS ONE

Words and Music by
Sy Oliver

But the technique we associate most strongly with bass lines is *walking*. By this, we mean constructing a mostly scalewise line that will convey the harmony. How do we do that? With any endeavor, the more rules we make, the more exceptions we are going to find, but we need to start somewhere. So, the first rule for walking bass lines is to *place roots on the downbeat*. Since much chord movement is by fourth or fifth, it works out that if we simply come down the scale from the root, we often end up on the root of the next chord without skipping a note:

Of course, we have to reverse the line at some point. To demonstrate that, let's start on D and go up with the same progression.

We began going up the scale, but we needed to skip a note in order to arrive at the root of the next chord on the downbeat.

With just these two patterns, 8-7-6-5 and 1-2-3-5, we can actually construct bass lines for almost any progression. Here are the first 16 measures of Jerome Kern's "The Way You Look Tonight":

THE WAY YOU LOOK TONIGHT

Words by Dorothy Fields
Music by Jerome Kern

When two chords come in the same measure, we can either treat them as if we were playing in two (measure 12) or use our repeated note technique (measure 13). If we have a chord that lasts more than a measure, we can use both the 1-2-3-5 and 8-7-6-5 patterns (measures 9 and 10), or continue the descending pattern for two measures, making it 8-7-6-5-4-3-2-1 (not shown).

The 1-2-3-5 and 8-7-6-5 patterns provide a reliable method for creating instant bass lines. It's a simple recipe, but it works. When combined with the techniques of playing in two and repeated notes, some very creative bass lines are possible.

After the rule to place roots on downbeats, our next concern is to *arrive at the root by stepwise motion, or (less common) by perfect fourth or perfect fifth.* The only reason for suggesting the 1-2-3-5 and 8-7-6-5 patterns was that they practically ensure that this will happen and they work for most chords. If the chord allows it, 1-2-3-♯3 can be used instead of 1-2-3-5:

So, could we also use 1-2-♭3-3 on the G⁷ and C⁶? We could, but the result would be different. Notice that by inserting B♭ into the line for G⁷, and E♭ for the C⁶, we place nonchord tones on the third beat.

Next to the downbeat, the third beat of the measure is the strongest. Whatever note lands on beat 3 is going to affect the character of the chord. So, in this case the G⁷ would take on a certain ♯9 quality and the C⁶ would sound a bit like a blues chord, since E♭ is the flatted third of the key. So, the next rule is, *place a chord tone on the third beat in most instances.* As for the 8-7-6-5 pattern, the sixth is such a common and noncommittal extension that it doesn't make any difference.

Before going on to more flexible patterns, we will use the 1-2-3-5 and 8-7-6-5 templates again to demonstrate how to adapt bass lines to minor keys:

For the most part, the key that you are in will govern note choices, not the upper structures that the chord might have. For example, normally a m7♭5 chord would receive a natural ninth as an upper structure, not a flat ninth. But in the bass line above, E♭ is the better choice, since it is the flatted third of the key (Cm).

Now let's use the three basic rules to construct some bass lines. To review:

1. Place roots on the downbeat.

2. Arrive at the root by stepwise motion, or (less common) by perfect fourth or perfect fifth.

3. Place a chord tone on the third beat in most instances.

Page 64 shows a bass line to Rhythm Changes, followed by a bass line to a chorus of blues. Notice how, in many instances, the downbeat is approached by a half step, even when the approach tone does not appear to belong to the harmony. The chromatic approach to the chord tone is very powerful. In most instances, it is better to approach by half step in preference to a chord tone a whole step away.

Latin Bass Lines

Latin bass lines can be very complex because there are many styles of Latin music, each calling for a different rhythm that is characteristic of the style. For this discussion, we will focus on the Bossa Nova, a form of Brazilian music with jazz influences that is often what American players are referring to when they call for a Latin beat.

Latin bass lines are about the rhythm more than the line. Figures are kept simple and repeated according to a beat that permeates the song. In its simplest terms, playing a Latin bass line means playing in two, but using a particular rhythm instead of half notes. As always, we want to break up the rhythm and the patterns occasionally. Below is a bass line for "Triste":

By Antonio Carlos Jobim

Another important Latin rhythm is the Rumba, which, in its simplest form, can be described as two dotted-quarter notes followed by a quarter note. This pattern can be elaborated on, and provides a basic starting point for many other types of Latin bass lines. Here is an example of a Rumba bass line:

Whether performing professionally, playing for enjoyment, or studying a tune's harmony, the bass line provides a powerful tool to bring the song to life. It is important to remember its function at all times—to provide a solid rhythmic background while communicating the chord structure. With that in mind, you can understand why strict rules do not apply—there are countless ways to do that. An effective bass line is not about choice of notes or choice of rhythmic pattern. It is about the total result. Once the patterns and basic concepts provided in this chapter have been absorbed, the reader is encouraged to experiment and be creative.

– CHAPTER 6 –
PLAYING THE CHORDS

"I always like people who have developed long and hard, especially through introspection and a lot of dedication. I think what they arrive at is usually a much deeper and more beautiful thing than the person who seems to have that ability and fluidity from the beginning." – **Bill Evans**

"It's taken me my whole life to learn what not to play." – **Dizzy Gillespie**

Basic Chording

This section will show you how to play some basic chords on the keyboard. One way of doing this is to sit at the piano and play a bass note in the left hand, along with the chord through the seventh in the right. Here are the first four measures of "There Is No Greater Love":

THERE IS NO GREATER LOVE

Words by Marty Symes
Music by Isham Jones

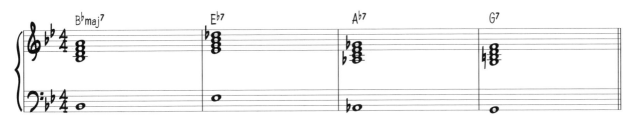

The harmony is clear, but this kind of playing is a little awkward, with the right hand skipping around so much. Since chord roots are being played in the left hand, there's no reason for the right hand to put the root in the bottom. Inverting the right-hand voicings will give a smoother voice leading:

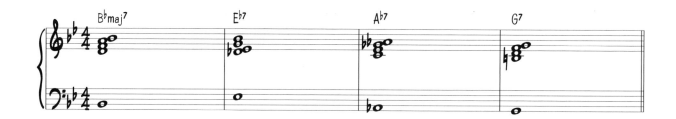

This approach is simple but effective. There are no rules as to how to do this, other than it's usually best if the fingers have to move very little to get to the next chord. For some styles of jazz, basic chording like this, with a bass line in the left hand, is all you need to back up a singer or horn player. (See Chapter 5, Bass Lines.)

Rhythmic Considerations

Next, we need to add some rhythm to our chords. There is a lot of freedom in how to do this, and pianists all have different styles. For pre-bebop styles, playing "straight four," with a chord on every beat, is a solid and appropriate rhythm. This is a standard comping technique for the guitar and a viable option for the piano as well.

Starting with bebop, most pianists became sparser with their chords. This style of comping can be summed up in four principles:

1. Most of the "hits" should be off the beat.

2. Give preference to anticipating the chord or beat, rather than delaying it.

3. Mix it up.

4. Leave some space.

Here are the chords to the first half of "Indiana (Back Home Again in Indiana)":

INDIANA
(Back Home Again In Indiana)

Words by Ballard MacDonald
Music by James F. Hanley

Dexterity in grabbing the basic sixth and seventh chords in all inversions is a valuable skill. Learning advanced voicings is fine (and necessary, for pianists), but taking shortcuts is not a good idea. It's best to build from the basics. That way, when you expand into more complex structures, you can experiment and develop your own voicings.

You'll notice that all the chords above contain the root and the fifth. If a bass line is provided—either by the left hand or by another instrument, these notes are not necessary. We may want to include them at times for reasons of color or voice leading, but we don't really need them.

Rootless Voicings

While there can be many ways to move from a basic seventh chord to chords that eliminate the root and fifth, we are going to have a look at the rootless voicings often associated with Bill Evans. These chords were initially developed as left-hand chords to accompany the right-hand improvisation, but they work equally well in the right hand when the left hand is providing the bass line. Normally, they hover somewhere around middle C. To be more specific, try to keep all the notes between third line bass clef and third line treble clef. Here is the formula:

- major chords   1-3-5-6 becomes 3-5-6-9 or 6-9-3-5
- minor seventhths   1-3-5-7 becomes 3-5-7-9 or 7-9-3-5
- dominant sevenths   1-3-5-7 becomes 3-13-7-9 or 7-9-3-13

Okay, let's look at what we have.

- major chords   9 replaces root
- minor sevenths   9 replaces root
- dominant sevenths   9 replaces root, 13 replaces 5

I have shown the major chord with a sixth, but the major seventh works equally well. Notice that all chords have either 3 or 7 in the bass. That way, when root motion is by fourth or fifth, we can just alternate inversions for smooth voice leading. Here's how that works for a ii–V^7–I progression:

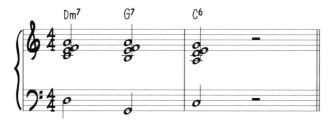

And if we were in a key somewhat removed in distance—say, F major—and wanted to stay in a similar range, beginning with the other inversion will do the trick:

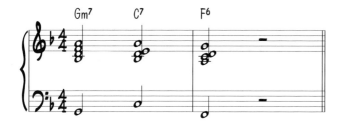

For the most part, this technique works with all chords. Minor sixth chords can be treated exactly like major sixth chords with a lowered third. Altered dominants can simply have the 9 or 13 adjusted to the desired note. But there are a few alterations we might want to make. To my ear, the m7♭5 chord has enough dissonance without the ninth. Moreover, the ninth of that chord is usually the natural third of the minor key that you're in, which sounds wrong to my ears. So, for a iim⁷♭⁵–V⁷–i cadence, here is a recommended option:

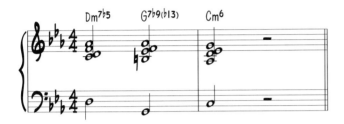

Diminished chords also require some special treatment. One approach is to substitute a dominant seventh chord for the diminished. In the example below, A⁷♭⁹, functioning as V⁷/ii, stands in for vii°⁷/ii. Notice that the ♭13 of the A⁷ (F natural) would not have been an option as an upper structure of the C♯°⁷. (Remember, a diminished chord can take any note a whole step above a chord member.)

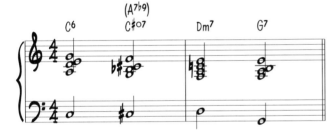

As an alternative, we can replace one or more members of the °7 with an upper structure. In the following example, A replaces G in the C♯°⁷:

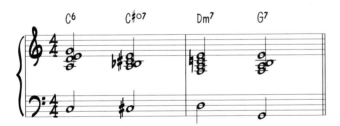

Below are the chords to part of "Indiana (Back Home Again in Indiana)," set with a bass line in the left hand and Bill Evans rootless chords in the right. Practically any tune in any real book can be played in similar fashion.

INDIANA
(Back Home Again In Indiana)

Words by Ballard MacDonald
Music by James F. Hanley

Two-Hand Voicings

When not playing the bass line or soloing, a pianist will usually play chords with both hands. If the root is going to be included in the chord, a very accessible way to do that is to place two notes in the left hand and three in the right, either in the configuration of 1-7-3-5-9 or 1-3-7-9-5:

This is a useful voicing, providing the four notes of the seventh chord (or sixth chord) along with one upper structure. For dominant chords, you could also replace the fifth with the 13th, and, of course, use whatever alterations of the ninth, fifth, or 13th that you need.

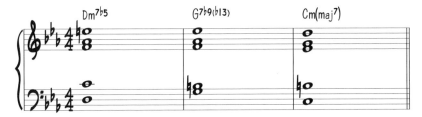

This voicing is excellent for browsing through a real book and getting a feel for the changes to a tune. The voicing is clear and unambiguous, and allows you to stop and experiment with upper structures or substitutions.

Below are the chords to the first half of "In a Mellow Tone," set with these voicings:

IN A MELLOW TONE

By Duke Ellington

While this lays down the chords clearly, it is probably not a voicing you'd want to use when playing with a rhythm section. When a bass line is already provided, playing the bass note deep in the left hand can get in the way and actually clash with what the bass player is doing. Just dropping the bass note isn't going to work either, because the left hand would be left with only one note. We need a voicing that will spread evenly across the two hands, picking up the crucial third and seventh and providing extensions.

Drop 2 Voicings

An excellent way to provide a solid, basic voicing is to take the Bill Evans rootless voicings and drop the second note from the top down an octave:

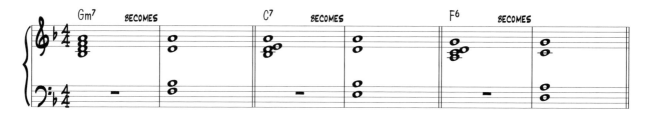

Or, with inversions:

As simple as it seems, this is a very effective comping voicing, conveying chord quality, transparency, and color. There are only four notes, but they're the right four, and the "fourthy" spacing yields a characteristic modern jazz sound. What's more, the notes easily fall under the fingers in a natural spacing that insures good voice leading. Just remember that the third, sixth, or seventh will always be in the bottom voice, which should normally be in the middle to upper part of the bass clef. (This voicing is so open that there is really a lot of flexibility. Range is seldom an issue.)

Here are Rhythm Changes set in Drop 2 voicings:

Voicings in Fourths

As an alternative to Drop 2 voicings, chords can be voiced in fourths, or predominantly fourths, by simply building from the bottom up and looking for the next available chord tone or extension approximately a fourth upward. A good way to start is to take the third and seventh as the bottom notes, add one more note in the left hand, and two more in the right. (You can also add a third note in the right hand, but we will limit this discussion to five-note voicings.) When chord motion is by fourth or fifth, as in a typical iim⁷–V⁷–I progression, the third and seventh will alternate as the lowest note:

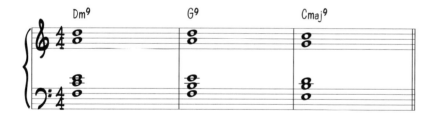

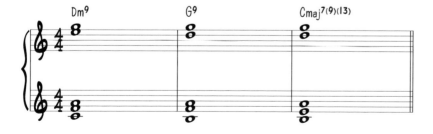

Just start with the third and seventh and continue upward using fourths, working in a third or fifth when necessary. Generally, the lowest note should be in this range:

The spacing of the chord is what makes it work, and you will need to adjust upper structures accordingly. This is demonstrated in the minor key examples that follow. First, note that the m7♭5 chord sounds better with the root or fifth in on the bottom. Also, to get a fourth-like sound, it's better to include the 11th but omit the ninth. On the dominant seventh, we include the ♭9, ♯9, and ♭13 because they are separated by fourths and allow us to get the desired spread for the chord. It is possible to mix and match other combinations involving the natural 9, natural 13, and ♯11.

In the alternative voicing below, we double the fifth of the Cm$^{6/9}$ in order to achieve the proper intervals. With these voicings, the spaces between the notes are as important as the notes themselves.

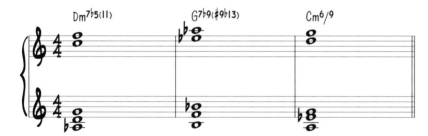

Diminished seventh chords present certain challenges in adapting them to a fourth based context since they are totally symmetrical and consist entirely of minor thirds. One way to do this is to limit the chord to a four-note structure and replace the seventh with the note a whole step higher:

The voicings shown above are just a few of hundreds that can be constructed along similar lines. You can and should experiment to find voicings that suit your taste.

Here is the first half of "In a Mellow Tone" voiced in fourths. (Upper structures are not indicated in the chord symbols.)

IN A MELLOW TONE

By Duke Ellington

— CHAPTER 7 —
PLAYING THE MELODY AND CHORDS TOGETHER

"Look, my songs are just tools for performing. Change it any way you want... so it works for you on the stage." – Harold Arlen

"When you know the lyrics to a tune, you have some kind of insight as to its composition. If you don't understand what it's about, you're depriving yourself of being really able to communicate this poem." – Dexter Gordon

Pianists have many options for playing the melody with chords for a song. Which option you choose depends on a variety of factors, including tempo, type of song, personal style, and skill level. And, of course, variety is important and a mixture of approaches to a song can add interest and inspire creativity. In this chapter, we will present several techniques that can be used to create a convincing rendition of the melody, suitable either for solo performance or playing with a rhythm section.

Ballad Playing

For slow songs, we could play straight seventh chords in the left hand with a single line melody in the right, but this approach is limited and fails to explore the extended possibilities of the keyboard. The left hand will be unable to reach for the necessary upper structures, while right hand is capable of more than just playing the melody. What we need to do is divide the responsibility between the two hands in a way that gives a nice spread to the notes of the chord but still allows the right hand to play the melody. Use of the damper pedal will help to connect the chords as well.

This chapter offers an approach to ballad playing that is not difficult and can be played by any musician who knows the chords and their extensions. You don't need big hands or a highly developed technique, but you do need to be able to find the chord tones quickly. Here are the principles:

1. The root, third, and seventh will always be present.

2. Upper structures will be added according to the guidelines given in Chapter 2.

3. The melody may serve as one of the required notes, though not usually in place of the root.

4. A five-note voicing is the norm, though fewer or more voices are possible.

5. Use larger intervals at the bottom and closer at the top. The root can be as deep in the bass as you can reach, but usually will fall within the bass clef staff.

With this method, the left hand will often have root and third as the lowest notes, or root and seventh. For major chords, root and fifth or root and sixth are also found. We will call the two lowest notes together the *bass voicing*. Here are the possible bass voicings:

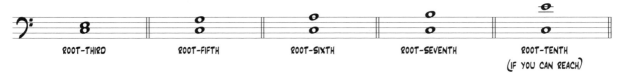

ROOT-THIRD   ROOT-FIFTH   ROOT-SIXTH   ROOT-SEVENTH   ROOT-TENTH
(IF YOU CAN REACH)

The tenth can be a helpful interval if you can reach it, but few men and fewer women can reach all the tenths, so it won't be included in this discussion.

You need to be careful with the root and third because it can sound muddy if set too low. That limit will depend on the keyboard you're playing. On a grand piano and most uprights, C-E is probably as low as you should go with a third.

Here is a ii–V⁷–I progression set with our ballad formula:

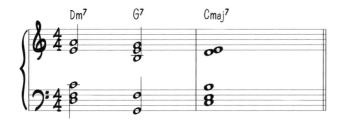

We had a few options in distributing our notes, but not many, assuming that the melody is fixed. While the Dm⁷ could receive a root-seventh bass voicing, with the third above that, a root-third bass voicing would not work well on the G⁷. G and B would be too close if placed at the bottom of the staff. If we put them an octave higher, we don't have room to open up the voicing of the chord. (When a chord is voiced in close position it is called a "block chord," which will be discussed later in this chapter.) Therefore, the bass voicings chosen are optimal for this progression, considering the placement of the melody.

Other than range issues, there is little to worry about. Overlapping of voicings with the melody is not a problem, so long as the hit is below the melody. After that, the melody may move into chord territory:

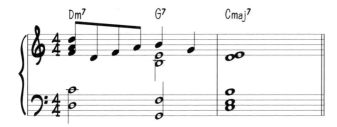

And we do need to observe chord symbols that call for bass notes other than the root:

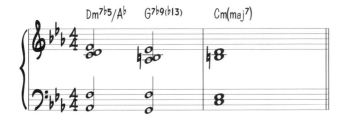

Below is a ballad setting of "They Didn't Believe Me." Notes should be distributed between the two hands comfortably, normally with the left hand covering notes through the range a seventh higher from the bass note and the right hand taking the rest.

THEY DIDN'T BELIEVE ME

Words by Herbert Reynolds
Music by Jerome Kern

Below is a ballad arrangement of "My Ship." The faster chord motion makes for a more interesting performance. This setting begins to explore some of the many things pianists to do enrich a ballad performance, such as the inner line movement on the sus chords, and the offbeat chord effect on the first two bars of the bridge.

MY SHIP

Words by Ira Gershwin
Music by Kurt Weill

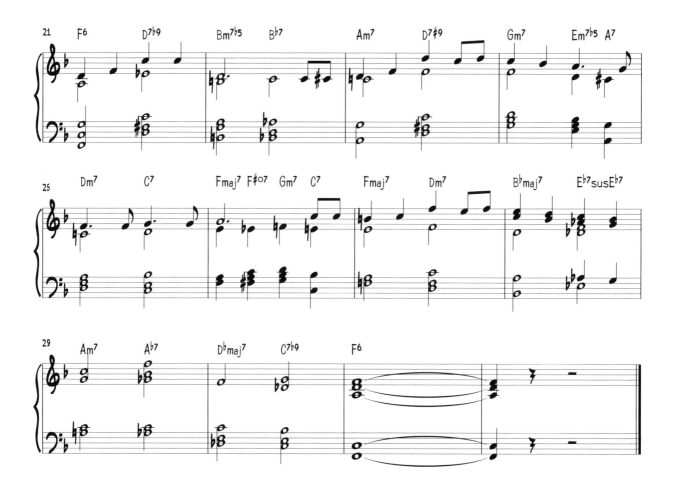

Swing and Bebop

As the tempo increases, we may find out our ballad approach no longer works. Basically, there are two problems that can occur. First, the steady unsyncopated rhythm does not give forward impetus to the song. Second, as the tempo increases, we find that the right hand may have to be totally devoted to playing the line, whether melody or improvisation, and cannot share in the chord playing. We have several options for faster tunes. One is to play a bass line in the left hand while the right hand plays the melody or improvises. (See Chapter 5, Bass Lines.) But the piano is a versatile instrument and we have several other options.

Bud Powell Voicings. When swing made the transition to bebop in the early 1940s, the role of the piano changed dramatically. More emphasis was placed on the improvised line, and the piano had to steer clear. That also applied to the pianist's own solos. Bud Powell's solution was to confine his solo comping to the left hand, playing sparse voicings that remained well below solo range. While Bud Powell sometimes used tenths and three-note structures in his comping, we will confine our version of these voicings to two-note voicings not involving the tenth. The formula is simple—each chord receives the root and either the third or seventh. (For a major sixth chord, use root and sixth.)

Here is the first half of "Scrapple from the Apple," with Bud Powell voicings as accompaniment:

SCRAPPLE FROM THE APPLE

By Charlie Parker

This technique is deliberately sparse and is best reserved for tunes that have a strong linear/harmonic component in the melody, such as bebop tunes, or improvisations to bebop tunes.

Latin Tunes

Latin tunes require a slightly different consideration. When you play Latin accompaniment on the keyboard it is best always to be thinking of the acoustic guitar. The comping should be light, rhythmically active but unobtrusive, dissonant yet transparent. Jobim, who was a pianist, also played the guitar, and approached the piano in a very subtle way.

Below is an arrangement of "The Girl from Ipanema," accompanied only by three-note chords in typical Bossa Nova rhythms. The chords are an adaptation of Bill Evans voicings using predominantly the third and seventh with one other note. Also, inversions are sometimes used that place notes other than the third or seventh in the bass. Notice that upper structures are often built into the melody. It is best to take advantage of them when choosing chord tones in order to avoid any kind of redundancy or heaviness.

THE GIRL FROM IPANEMA
(GARÔTA DE IPANEMA)

Music by Antonio Carlos Jobim
English Words by Norman Gimbel
Original Words by Vinicius de Moraes

Block Chords

One option for harmonizing a melody is to play parallel chords, with all voices moving in rhythm with the melody. This is known as block chords, or locked hands style. It is a very rich and heavy sound, and best reserved for portions of tunes. Pioneered by Milt Buckner, the technique became closely associated with George Shearing, and it is his method that we will begin with. Keep in mind that Shearing and others took a very flexible and creative approach to block chords, and their nuances are beyond the scope of this book. What I will provide is a straightforward approach to block chords that will be effective in many contexts.

In essence, we want to fill in all the notes of the chord immediately below the melody in the right hand and double the melody in the left. Here are the root, third, fifth, and sixth notes of an F⁶ with block chords beneath them:

We could have used an Fmaj⁷ to harmonize A, C, or E, but we really wouldn't want to use it on the F, since it would create a half step between the upper voices.

So what do we do with the other notes in the scale? We could just fill them in with diatonic chords—and at times we will want to do that, but a more dynamic approach is to harmonize them with diminished seventh chords. Here is an F major scale set that way:

All you have to remember to do for non-chord tones is build a diminished chord on the note itself. It works whether ascending or descending, in both scalar and angular passages.

The same principles apply to other chords, but we sometimes need to be flexible with the formula. Here are the first seven bars of "They Didn't Believe Me":

THEY DIDN'T BELIEVE ME

Words by Herbert Reynolds
Music by Jerome Kern

Notice how the chord does not change when tied between bars 1 and 2. The whole idea of block chords is that the harmony changes when the melody changes, and not vice versa. However, there is nothing wrong with repeating the same voicing if the melody note changes (bars 2 and 4). Also, when block chording ii–V progressions, it is often a good idea to go back and forth between ii and V freely, rather than compartmentalizing them.

Chromatic (nondiatonic) tones in the melody require special treatment, but we have several options. Often, a diminished chord will work, but in general we want to avoid consecutive diminished chords (the old silent movie effect). One alternative is to put a diatonic chord on the scale note that would normally receive a diminished chord (beat 3 below):

Another possibility is to use a dominant seventh built on the chromatic note (beat 2 below):

Since block chord style typically allows only four notes, we can't always incorporate all the upper structures called for by the harmony. In that case, we choose what we believe will be the most effective notes. Sometimes, we will elect to eliminate the root or fifth of a dominant chord to make room for upper structures. Below are the first eight measures of "My Ship," set in block chords. Note how the dominant chords sometimes have the root omitted. Also, observe that when minor seventh chords have the 11th in the melody, the third is often left out.

MY SHIP

Words by Ira Gershwin
Music by Kurt Weill

Melodies that have continuous motion lend themselves to block chording. When they don't, we sometimes need to fill in some notes to keep the momentum going, as in this version of "There Will Never Be Another You." (In the example that follows, some notes have been indicated in the bass clef for clarity, but, as always, the upper four notes are to be played in the right hand.)

THERE WILL NEVER BE ANOTHER YOU

Lyric by Mack Gordon
Music by Harry Warren

Drop 2 Voicing is a technique that derives from block chords. (See discussion of Drop 2 Voicings in Chapter 6.) As the name implies, the second line from the top is dropped an octave. The melody is not doubled. Here is "Bye Bye Blackbird" in Drop 2.

BYE BYE BLACKBIRD

Lyric by Mort Dixon
Music by Ray Henderson

Although it involves only four voices, Drop 2 is a more difficult technique because you need to keep track of the second voice and drop it down into the left hand. The style is open to advanced techniques and procedures and has been explored at great length by Kenny Barron, McCoy Tyner, Barry Harris, and others.

Stride

Stride is a technique in which the right hand plays the melody or improvises while the left hand alternates between the bass notes and the chords. The name derives from the leaping motion the left hand engages in while carrying out its task. Stride reached its pinnacle in the 1920s, when the masters such as James P. Johnson, Willie "The Lion" Smith, and Fats Waller played with a brilliance that has never been surpassed. As many recordings indicate, a competent stride pianist can serve as the entire rhythm section in driving a band. Here is an example of how a Harlem Stride pianist might play the first measures of Rhythm Changes:

When you consider that the right hand would also be busy improvising, all done at breakneck tempo, this is not a pursuit for the faint of heart.

With the rise of electronic recording and use of microphones and pick-ups, bass players became more prominent and piano players began to stay out of their way. The use of stride piano with a band became rare after the 1920s, as the role of the piano became more subtle and less obtrusive. But stride never went away. Many players continued to use the technique in their solo playing as a versatile expressive tool. (Oscar Peterson and George Shearing, for example, were masters of the style.)

As indicated above, my definition of stride is a broad one, indicating any accompaniment style where the left hand plays the bass note on one beat and a chord on the next. I reserve the term Harlem Stride to refer to the virtuosic style of the 1920s, which obviously wasn't intended for nonpianists. But the basic *concept* of stride piano was *not* too hard for the average player, and was in fact very common in typical sheet music arrangements.

Below is the opening from the published sheet music to George M. Cohan's "Give My Regards to Broadway." Notice how the left hand plays a bass note on beats 1 and 3 and the chord on beats 2 and 4.

GIVE MY REGARDS TO BROADWAY

Words and Music by
George M. Cohan

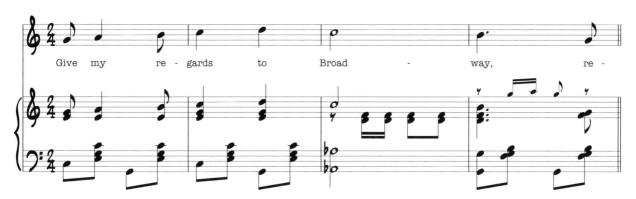

There are no rules about how to voice or invert the chord on the offbeats. The above example puts the tonic chord in first inversion and the dominant chord in third inversion with the fifth omitted. But in the example that follows (the chorus to "Rose Room"), the fifth of the dominant seventh is on the bottom for the first chord and the root for the second. Also, note that the bass note may be doubled to make it more prominent.

ROSE ROOM

Words by Harry Williams
Music by Art Hickman

The upshot is that it's all about range. You need to stay out of the way of the melody, but at the same time keep the chord high enough so it doesn't sound muddy. A good rule of thumb is to keep the left hand little finger somewhere around fourth line F in the bass clef and invert the chord accordingly.

Here is a stride version of "They Didn't Believe Me." As with any approach or technique, too much of one thing can wear thin. It's a good idea to mix things up on occasion with at least a passing bass note or connecting chord (see measures 8 and 23).

THEY DIDN'T BELIEVE ME

Words by Herbert Reynolds
Music by Jerome Kern

I've written the melody as a single line, which is probably enough of a challenge for a nonpianist when tackling stride. Experienced pianists usually flesh out the melody by playing it an octave higher and "blocking" the chord beneath it. The formula is simple: keeping the right hand within an octave, add one, two, or three chord tones underneath. Don't try to block every single note. Just try to support prominent melody notes and changes of harmony. Let your note choices be guided by what will be a comfortable hand position for you.

Here's an example of blocking:

The following stride version of "After You've Gone" uses octaves for the downbeats of the bass notes, making it somewhat more challenging to perform, but adding a richer sound. Also, we can leave the root out of the chord on occasion, since it is already provided by the bass. Similarly, if an upper structure is provided by the melody, such as in measure 5, we may wish to leave it out of the chord voicing.

AFTER YOU'VE GONE

Words by Henry Creamer
Music by Turner Layton

For a more dissonant sound, we can actually employ our Bill Evans rootless voicings, although we may need to adjust the inversion and be content to stay in the proper range. Below is "Gee Baby, Ain't I Good to You." Notice the inversions where notes other than the third or seventh are on the bottom. Again, sometimes we allow the melody to complete the chord (measure 12):

GEE BABY, AIN'T I GOOD TO YOU

Words by Don Redman and Andy Razaf
Music by Don Redman

Combining Techniques

To add interest, especially on ballads and medium tempo tunes, we want to play something other than sustained chords and melody. Following are three arrangements that employ typical pianistic techniques to achieve this. Notice how the right hand sometimes moves independently of the left and vice versa. Here are ideas for building more interesting keyboard settings of tunes, along with where examples can be found in the settings below.

- Modified stride bass ("My Buddy," opening measures) with damper pedal

- Broken chords ("My Buddy," measure 17)

- Left-hand bass with right-hand chords under melody
  ("Beyond the Sea," opening measures)

- Punctuated chording ("Beyond the Sea" opening measures)

- Contrast between two-beat and walking bass patterns ("Beyond the Sea")

- Two-hand melody and accompaniment moving together
  ("Alice in Wonderland," opening measures)

- Varying basic harmonies with more complex chords
  ("Alice in Wonderland" first 16 measures contrasted with following section)

- Pedal tone ("Alice in Wonderland," measure 33)

- Inner melodic lines ("Alice in Wonderland," measures 41–44)

- Rhythmic variation in left-hand chording ("Alice in Wonderland," measure 49)

- Sometimes inner voice movement implies harmonies that are too intricate
  to be captured by chord symbols ("Alice in Wonderland," measure 50)

Ideas could be adapted for guitar? I think so, so I do so as part of my comping studies

MY BUDDY

Lyrics by Gus Kahn
Music by Walter Donaldson

BEYOND THE SEA

Lyrics by Jack Lawrence
Music by Charles Trenet and Albert Lasry
Original French Lyric to "La Mer" by Charles Trenet

ALICE IN WONDERLAND

Words by Bob Hilliard
Music by Sammy Fain

– CHAPTER 8 –
IMPROVISATION

"You've got to learn your instrument. Then, you practice, practice,
practice. And then, when you finally get up there on the bandstand,
forget all that and just wail." **– Charlie Parker**

"My theory is never to discard the melody." **– Jelly Roll Morton**

Basic Improvisation

This chapter will present some guidelines for improvising solos on the chord changes
to songs found in real books. To try to turn improvisation into an exact science with
precise rules would be contradictory to the very meaning of the term. Improvisation
is about playing what you feel, not planning your moves, and playing what comes into
your ear. Nevertheless, a reasonable question for someone who has never done it is,
"How do I get started?"

You start with the melody. If you look at the development of jazz historically, you
find that the early practitioners began by embellishing the melody. Even when the
music became more advanced, the master players tended to keep the melody in
the background when they played, referring to it occasionally and playing a solo in
keeping with the character of the original tune. (Lester Young was particularly skilled
at this.)

Sure, there may be tunes or jazz heads that don't offer much in the way of melody, or
times when someone says, "Let's play some blues." But even in such cases, a master
improviser will grab onto some phrase or idea at the beginning and work with it. The
point is that you want to improvise a cohesive solo, one that makes sense. Improvising
is about creating a whole, not about knocking out chord changes one by one like
you're playing some kind of video game.

A self-evident approach to improvising would be simply to play the chords as
arpeggios. While too much of this approach would turn a piece into a mere study
exercise, it can be a creative tool in building inventive solos when used sparingly.
But there are some restrictions. In jazz improvisation, some chords can be played
as arpeggios and some cannot.

 Direct spellings of minor seventh chords, minor 7♭5 chords, diminished chords, and
augmented chords all provide acceptable lines. Major and dominant chords, however,
should not be directly spelled from the root. Doing so emphasizes the wrong notes in
the chord and gives an uncharacteristic sound.

Here is a list of common seventh chords as arpeggios:

Additionally, any chord can be arpeggiated starting from the third in a 3-5-7-9 configuration:

When descending, there are no restrictions. Any chord played in a 7-5-3-1 pattern makes an acceptable line.

Guide Tone Approach

I'm going to suggest what is generally called the "guide tone" approach to improvisation. This is by no means the only way to improvise. There are many different approaches, some of which achieve the same result, and some of which have different goals entirely. But the guide tone approach provides a straightforward way of improvising lines that carry the harmony and sound like classic "straight-ahead" playing. More than that, this method is flexible, and can be used to play Dixieland as well as very dissonant "outside" styles.

Guide tones are the notes that define and distinguish the chord. (Note that I am using the term to refer to structural tones, which is slightly different from the concept of "guide tone lines" used by arrangers.) It is not always an easy call as to which tones are guide tones and which ones are not, and all players are not in agreement. (That's a good thing, and it's part of the reason we all hear differently and have different styles.) But clearly, some notes in a chord are more important than others. The third and seventh are usually guide tones. The fifth and ninth may be considered guide tones if flatted. The root is generally not considered a guide tone, except in the case of tonic chords.

Chord Type	Guide Tones
Cmaj7 or C6	C, E
Cm7	E♭, B♭
Cm7♭5	E♭, G♭, B♭
C7♭9	E, B♭, D♭

There is little difference in how an improviser will treat a maj7 or a maj6/9, other than possibly giving the maj7 more emphasis if that note is in the chord. They are basically the same.

In the guide tone approach to improvisation, we emphasize crucial notes by placing them on strong beats (1 and 3), downbeats of strong measures, points of harmonic change, leaping to or away from them, or by shaping the line so that the guide tones are targeted.

To make this happen, we measure our steps so that we land on the target note. Just as a base runner will increase or decrease the size of his steps to make sure he steps on the bag, so will the improviser use the necessary intervals to make sure a guide tone occurs on the intended beat. But in improvising, we also have the option of encircling the note—of going past it, and perhaps back and forth a few times, before landing on it.

In the passage above, notice how beat 2 has an eighth note below and above the C on beat 3. We could actually reverse these notes and the effect would be the same. Coming from the G on beat 4, a half step allows us to hit the F on the downbeat of measure 2. From there, we simply play down the scale to place the B on beat 3. The A♭ on the G7, also a guide tone, is given prominence—not by placing it on a downbeat, but by skipping into it by a large interval.

In the following illustration, we can see that if we remove all the upbeats, looking at just the downbeats, we have all chord tones. (C6 usually represents C6/9, so the D is a chord tone.):

A master improviser does these things naturally, without thinking about them. It all has to do with hearing lines that sound interesting and at the same time reveal the chord sequence.

Below is an improvised solo to "If I Were a Bell," with the melody included below for comparison. Notice:

- The melody is referred to periodically.

- Guide tones appear in prominent places.

- Chords are not in airtight boxes. Lines can spill over into the next chord.

- iim^7 and V^7 chords tend to blend together. The improvised line can treat either one (measures 8, 24).

- Passing chords may be played (as in measure 26) or completely ignored (as in measures 27–28).

- The preferred note to give impetus to the line takes priority over the exact chord tone (E natural on F^7 in measures 9, 11, and 25).

- A short tonic area can be treated as a I chord and intervening chords ignored (measures 15–16).

- Blue notes are permissible (measure 15).

- The difference between a maj7 and a maj6 is not reflected in the improvised line (measure 3).

- Upper structures, including altered ones, can be added to chords freely (measure 18).

Joe Pass only looked @ m X

IF I WERE A BELL

By Frank Loesser

When the harmonic motion is fast, and chords are coming rapidly, chords need to be "spelled" with the utmost clarity. In particular, we need to emphasize the guide tones and be careful of too many extensions. If we are playing eighth notes and the chords come every two beats, we have only four notes to spell each chord, so we need to choose carefully. This is demonstrated in the solo on "Giant Steps" that follows. Notice that many of the chords begin on the root and the entire triad is often present.

GIANT STEPS

By John Coltrane

To improvise such solos at fast tempos, the patterns need to be prepared in advance. Listening to John Coltrane's solo on this tune, it is clear that he had done his homework and had a cache of devices worked out and ready to go. I've tried to avoid those patterns in the above solo in order to demonstrate that there are many possibilities to be explored. And once you've worked out your original patterns, they can be modified and combined in many ways. The point is, even a set of chord changes that boxes you in with tight harmonic constraints still allows for a vast amount of creativity and exploration.

But sometimes we want to go completely in the opposite direction—to play lyrical solos, avoiding stock patterns and methodical chord running. Latin tunes usually suggest such an approach. Here is a solo on the first half of "Wave." Notice how the melody is kept mostly intact, and improvisational passages are often variations or manipulations of the tune itself. Latin tunes lend themselves to creative rhythms (measures 5–6 and 14–19). With tunes that are rhythmically active, we usually want to do more than just play a steady stream of eighth notes.

WAVE

Words and Music by
Antonio Carlos Jobim

The Blues

The blues and jazz originated from the same sources at approximately the same time, and the two have been inextricably interwoven ever since. A jazz musician does not wait for a 12-bar blues number to interject a blues feel into a song, nor does a tune that's called a blues require a different approach to improvisation. Blues is a concept and a feeling that manifests itself in melodic and rhythmic choices that are always available to the improviser. Even Bossa Nova tunes use blue notes.

While any note can be manipulated in the blues, the most frequent choices are the third and seventh, with the fifth not far behind. The difference is, however, that the seventh remains flatted, while the third and fifth will either be bent (by a vocalist or guitarist) or juxtaposed (by an instrument with fixed pitches). In a harmonic context, the inclusion of these notes in a major chord gives us the "Jimi Hendrix Chord," the $V^{7\sharp9}$. This chord was actually in use by jazz musicians decades before Hendrix popularized it, and clearly owes its origins to the blues.

This chord is not always used as a blues chord—it can also function as a standard dominant seventh with added dissonance. When used as a blues chord, it will represent the tonic chord and will frequently appear in vamps.

If we take the commonly altered notes in the blues and superimpose them over a traditional European major scale, we get this:

Keep in mind that there is no specific "blues scale," although it is indeed possible to string blue notes together into scalar passages. Here is a common one:

This exact sequence of notes appears in measures 14 and 15 of "Wave" in descending form:

Although this collection of notes offers a quick method of playing passages with a blues flavor, it is somewhat confining, and omits other important notes in the scale—in particular, the natural third, sixth, and second. Additionally, it emphasizes the ♭5, which is not nearly as common as the ♭3 and ♭7 in blues performance. A way around that difficulty is to use a "minor" pentatonic scale, which consists of the following notes:

This scale is actually very important in that it (or something very close to this) is found in the indigenous music of musical cultures throughout the world. The term "pentatonic" simply implies that the scale has five notes. But in Western music, the term always refers to this scale or a transposition of this scale.

With these tools, it should be possible to construct a variety of blues passages:

Blues was invented out of an aural tradition, so obviously the best way to learn the blues is to listen to it. The historic recordings of Bessie Smith and Ma Rainey will give a good indication of the origins of the blues. And, of course, the great jazz instrumentalists, such as Louis Armstrong and Charlie Parker, were deeply rooted in the blues.

An important point to keep in mind with the blues it that the altered notes apply to the overall key, not to the chord of the moment. Also, blue notes, being so strongly tied to the very roots of jazz, tend to push other chords out of the way. It is not at all uncommon for an improviser to start playing blues phases and completely ignore the changing harmonies.

Finally, as was mentioned in the chapter on form, all blues tunes are not necessarily 12-bar structures, just as some 12-bar "blues" structures have very little blues character. An excellent example of a blues-flavored jazz tune that is not a 12-bar blues is "Doxy." Notice that the melody makes extensive use of the both the natural and flat third, as well as the sixth (measures 10 and 11). A tune such as this one offers a broad range of possibilities for the improviser, everything from running every change to ignoring every change and simply blowing some blues licks in B♭. The master improviser will combine both, instilling the tune with a blues flavor while punctuating the solo with well placed guide tones.

DOXY

By Sonny Rollins

When to Ignore the Changes

Even when not specifically playing blues licks, you don't need to improvise over every single chord change. There is nothing at all wrong with simply ignoring some of the passing chords and improvising freely in the key that you are in, even though the improvised line will appear to clash with the chord being played at that moment. The passages below contain perfectly acceptable improvised passages that do not follow the moving chords behind them. They may look wrong to the eye, but they sound perfectly fine, and are similar to countless such passages found in the recorded solos of the finest improvisers.

There would be nothing wrong with catching every single chord in such passages, but it actually suggests a higher level of creativity to improvise within the key and ignore the embellishing chords. This less-is-more approach was typical of masters such as Lester Young and Miles Davis.

Vocabulary

Vocabulary is an essential part of improvisation. Lester Young used to say that a solo should "tell a story." To tell a story, you need ideas and musical experiences to share with the audience. That's why it is important to listen extensively and to learn the standards, both popular and jazz. Other kinds of music can also enrich a musician's vocabulary. Classical, country, rock and roll, hip hop—all have all rubbed shoulders with jazz and left an impact. A jazz musician with broad listening experiences is an interesting storyteller.

– CHAPTER 9 –
REHARMONIZATION

"Play the vanilla changes." – Lester Young

"The wise musicians are those who play what they can master."
– Duke Ellington

Reharmonization refers to changing the chords to a song—either adding chords, removing chords, or substituting other chords. Specifically, the term "substitution" should apply only to the replacement of chords, while "reharmonization" should refer to any and all changes made to the harmony. But in practice, the words are used interchangeably.

Although extensive reharmonization is often necessary with a fake book, the chords in a real book tend to be much more reliable. But reliable does not mean original, and it is important to realize that, for many standard songs, the chords are already reharmonized. Seldom do the chords in the original sheet music reflect what the composer intended, let alone what a jazz musician would play.

George Gershwin describes the situation in his introduction to *Gershwin at the Keyboard:*

> Sheet music, as ordinarily printed for mass sales, is arranged with an eye
> to simplicity. The publishers cannot be blamed for getting out simplified
> versions of songs, since the majority of the purchasers of popular music
> are little girls with little hands, who have not progressed very far in their
> study of the piano.

Since the chords are not original anyway, there is ample justification for creating your own, either for variety, to accommodate the musicians performing the music, to adapt the music to a specific style, or just for reasons of personal taste. Here follow a few basic principles that can be used to add different chords to a tune

Diatonic Substitution

As was mentioned, the seven diatonic chords can be divided into three groups: tonic (Imaj^7, iiim^7, vim^7), pre-dominant (iim^7 and IVmaj^7) and dominant (V^7 and vii^{o7}). Any of these chords can substitute for others in the group. For example:

B♭maj^7	E♭maj^7	F^7	B♭maj^7	can become	Dm^7	E♭maj^7	F^7	Gm^7
Imaj^7	IVmaj^7	V^7	Imaj^7		iiim^7	IVmaj^7	V^7	vim^7

Diatonic substitution also works for secondary functions or tonicizations (see Chapter 2):

$B\flat^6$	G^7	Cm^7	F^7	can become	$B\flat^6$	B^{o7}	Cm^7	F^7
I^6	V^7/ii	iim^7	V^7		I^6	vii^{o7}/ii	iim^7	V^7

Since the diatonic functions of V^7 and vii^{o7} are equivalent, we have simply substituted one for the other. V^7/any chord = vii^{o7}/any chord.

Dominant Interchange

Melody and context permitting, any straight dominant chord can be preceded by its related iim^7, and any iim^7–V^7 progression can have the iim^7 removed. For example, a rhythm bridge in $B\flat$ can be either

D^7	G^7	C^7	F^7

or

Am^7	D^7	Dm^7	G^7	Gm^7	C^7	Cm^7	F^7

Typically, pre-bebop tunes tend to use straight dominant sevenths, while bebop tunes lean toward iim^7–V^7s.

Added ii–Vs

These chords will precede and target a specific chord, and may either be inserted or replace existing chords.

C^6	Dm^7	G^7	Am	becomes	C^6	Dm^7	Bm^7	E^7	Am
I^6	iim^7	V^7	vim		I^6	iim^7	iim^7	V^7	i
								vim	

The iim^7–V^7 of Am replaces the original V^7.

Added Diminished Chords

We've seen ascending diminished chords connect two chords a whole step apart by acting as vii^{o7} of the second chord, but diminished chords can descend by half step as well. Diminished seventh chords have a long history as connecting chords. They can be inserted to connect chords that are a whole step apart.

Em^7	Dm^7	G^7	becomes	Em^7	$E\flat^{o7}$	Dm^7	G^7

Diminished chords can also act as lead-in chords. For example:

becomes:

I've written the chord in root position to show its function as vii°⁷/V⁷, but in practice, many swing and Dixieland musicians would play a C°⁷ in this situation. Either inversion will work.

Added Diatonic Passing Chords

Diatonic chords do not have to function harmonically. They can also "walk," by simply moving up or down the scale.

Cmaj⁷ G⁷   becomes Cmaj⁷ Dm⁷ Em⁷ Fmaj⁷ G⁷

Descending Chromatic Minor Seventh Chords

It is common for minor seventh chords to descend chromatically. This presents an opportunity for substitution whenever another chord intervenes between two minor seventh chords a whole step apart:

Em⁷ A⁷ Dm⁷ G⁷ becomes Em⁷ E♭m⁷ Dm⁷ G⁷

Side Stepping

A short progression (usually or two chords) can abruptly shift up or down a half step and then back to the original:

Dm⁷ G⁷ becomes Dm⁷ G⁷ E♭m⁷ A♭⁷ Dm⁷ G⁷

This is what is done on p. 23, not tritone sub as shown here ↓

Tritone Substitution

Substitute the dominant chord a tritone away from the original (See the explanation in Chapter 2). Tritone subs can also be preceded by their related iim7 chord:

Cmaj⁷ Gm⁷ C⁷ Fmaj⁷ becomes Cmaj⁷ D♭m⁷ G♭⁷ Fmaj⁷

Chord Quality Change

Sometimes a chord will be substituted that has a different quality from the one expected on that function. The expectation is that the root will suggest the harmonic movement while the upper notes provide color. This is often done with tritone substitutions. For example:

Dm^7	Db^7	$Cmaj^7$	becomes	Dm^7	$Dbmaj^7$	$Cmaj^7$
iim^7	$subV^7$	$Imaj^7$		iim^7	$bIImaj^7$	$Imaj^7$

Counter-melodies

Sometimes it is possible to suggest a counter-melody through changing extensions or chord types. In such circumstances, the functional harmony remains basically unchanged, but the quality of the seventh or extensions changes in a recognizable pattern. For example, take the opening of "That Old Black Magic," which begins with six measures of Eb:

THAT OLD BLACK MAGIC

Words by Johnny Mercer
Music by Harold Arlen

That's a long time to play on one chord. We could easily enough add iim^7–V^7s, tritone subs, or other chords, but we probably don't want to do that. Here are lyrics to the first part of the song:

"That old black magic has me in its spell, that old black magic that you weave so well."

The whole point of the hovering melody and unchanging harmony is to convey the feeling of being "spellbound." We don't want to destroy that by turning the tune into something it wasn't intended to be.

But there is another way we can add interest. It is possible to set up a countermelody by changing the sevenths or upper structures of the chords in a patterned way:

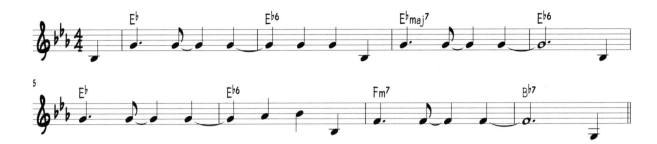

Now, as the other notes in the chords remain the same, the changing notes suggest this melody:

These internal melodies that follow inside voices are sometimes called "line clichés," or, if you want to be fancy, CESH (Contrapuntal Elaboration of Static Harmony). But fancy terminology is unnecessary because the concept is simple and straightforward. Several common chord sequences allow for such melodies, including this common minor chord progression from "In a Sentimental Mood":

IN A SENTIMENTAL MOOD

By Duke Ellington

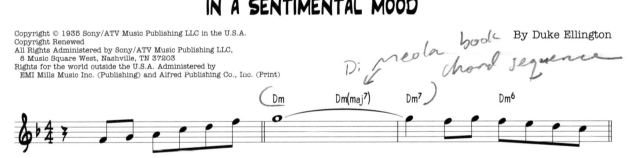

The chords suggest the descending line D-C♯-C-B, which may be played either in the bass or in another voice. Extended tonic minor chords often allow for this progression.

Final Thoughts on Reharmonization

It is easy to overdo it when reharmonizing, and "less is more" is always good musical advice. Many improvisers feel that too many chords crowd them, taking away choices they would rather make for themselves. Since many of the chords you see are already reharmonizations, there may actually be cases where you'd want to remove some chords or extensions. Remember, "interesting" all the time is boring!

ACKNOWLEDGMENTS

I would like to thank all those who assisted me with this project. Special gratitude to my wife, Nancy Rawlins, who worked closely with me every step of the way; to Jon Barnes, who reviewed the manuscript; to Carl Hausman, who assisted in editing the prose; to Ed Wise, who's always there to answer my questions; to my colleague Denis DiBlasio, for sharing his ideas and approaches to jazz; and to George Mesterhazy, one of my favorite musicians and a lifelong mentor and friend.

ABOUT THE AUTHOR

Robert Rawlins is a professor and coordinator of music theory at Rowan University in Glassboro, New Jersey. He is the author of five books and more than 100 articles on various aspects of music theory, jazz, history, and performance. As a woodwind player, Rawlins has performed extensively, including engagements with the Philly Pops, various stage shows in Atlantic City and elsewhere, Philadelphia theaters, and jazz clubs. He recently spent a year in New Orleans, studying and performing early jazz. Rawlins attended Berklee College of Music and holds graduate degrees from Rowan University, California State University, and Rutgers University, where he received a Ph.D. in musicology.

The Best-Selling Jazz Book of All Time Is Now Legal!

The Real Books are the most popular jazz books of all time. Since the 1970s, musicians have trusted these volumes to get them through every gig, night after night. The problem is that the books were illegally produced and distributed, without any regard to copyright law, or royalties paid to the composers who created these musical masterpieces.

Hal Leonard is very proud to present the first legitimate and legal editions of these books ever produced. You won't even notice the difference, other than all the notorious errors being fixed: the covers and typeface look the same, the song lists are nearly identical, and the price for our edition is even cheaper than the originals!

Every conscientious musician will appreciate that these books are now produced accurately and ethically, benefitting the songwriters that we owe for some of the greatest tunes of all time!

Real Book 1-5
Rock Book 1+2

VOLUME 1
00240221	C Edition	$32.50
00240224	B♭ Edition	$32.50
00240225	E♭ Edition	$32.50
00240226	Bass Clef Edition	$32.50
00240292	C Edition 6 x 9	$27.95
00451087	C Edition on CD-ROM	$25.00
00240302	A-D Play-Along CDs	$24.99
00240303	E-J Play-Along CDs	$24.95
00240304	L-R Play-Along CDs	$24.95
00240305	S-Z Play-Along CDs	$24.99

VOLUME 2
00240222	C Edition	$29.99
00240227	B♭ Edition	$32.50
00240228	E♭ Edition	$32.50
00240229	Bass Clef Edition	$32.50
00240293	C Edition 6 x 9	$27.95
00240351	A-D Play-Along CDs	$24.99
00240352	E-I Play-Along CDs	$24.99
00240353	J-R Play-Along CDs	$24.99
00240354	S-Z Play-Along CDs	$24.99

VOLUME 3
00240233	C Edition	$32.50
00240284	B♭ Edition	$29.95
00240285	E♭ Edition	$29.95
00240286	Bass Clef Edition	$29.95

VOLUME 4
00240296	C Edition	$29.99

VOLUME 5
00240349	C Edition	$32.50

Also available:
00240264	The Real Blues Book	$34.99
00310910	The Real Bluegrass Book	$29.99
00240137	Miles Davis Real Book	$19.95
00240355	The Real Dixieland Book	$29.99
00240235	The Duke Ellington Real Book	$19.99
00240358	The Charlie Parker Real Book	$19.99
00240331	The Bud Powell Real Book	$19.99
00240313	The Real Rock Book	$29.99
00240359	The Real Tab Book – Vol. 1	$32.50
00240317	The Real Worship Book	$29.99

THE REAL CHRISTMAS BOOK
00240306	C Edition	$25.00
00240345	B♭ Edition	$25.00
00240346	E♭ Edition	$25.00
00240347	Bass Clef Edition	$25.00
00240431	A-G Play-Along CDs	$24.99
00240432	H-M Play-Along CDs	$24.99
00240433	N-Y Play-Along CDs	$24.99

THE REAL VOCAL BOOK
00240230	Volume 1 High Voice	$29.95
00240307	Volume 1 Low Voice	$29.99
00240231	Volume 2 High Voice	$29.95
00240308	Volume 2 Low Voice	$29.99
00240391	Volume 3 High Voice	$29.99
00240392	Volume 3 Low Voice	$29.99

THE REAL BOOK – STAFF PAPER
00240327		$9.95

HOW TO PLAY FROM A REAL BOOK
For All Musicians
by Robert Rawlins
00312097		$14.99

Complete song lists online at www.halleonard.com
Prices and availability subject to change without notice.